The Epistle of Paul the Apostle to the Galatians

by
Oliver B. Greene

THE GOSPEL HOUR, INC.
Oliver B. Greene, Founder
Box 2024, Greenville, South Carolina 29602

© Copyright 1962 by Oliver B. Greene
All rights reserved
Printed in the United States of America

First printing, December 1962 — 10,000 copies
Second printing, January 1964 — 10,000 copies
Third printing, January 1966 — 10,000 copies
Fourth printing, July 1969 — 15,000 copies
Fifth printing, December 1971 — 15,000 copies
Sixth printing, November 1973 — 15,000 copies
Seventh printing, April 1975 — 25,000 copies
Eighth printing, June 1977 — 15,000 copies
Ninth printing, March 1984 — 10,000 copies

PREFACE

The Law and The Gospel do not keep company. They do not walk together because they are not agreed. They are by nature as far apart as the East is from the West--and I do not believe you have ever heard of an "East pole" and a "West pole." The Law and the Gospel are by nature as far apart as life and death. The one (The Law) is the ministry of death. The other (The Gospel) is the ministry of life. The Law is the whip-lash of the Judgment of Almighty God. God thundered out, "The soul that sinneth shall surely die!" Sin is the transgression of God's Law.

The Gospel of the marvelous grace of God--the Good News of salvation--is a silver bell ringing out the anthem of God's indescribable love. The Law provides a work to be done . . . the Law says "Do." The Gospel presents a Word to be believed . . . "Faith cometh by hearing, and hearing by the Word." "He that heareth my Word and believeth on Him that sent me hath everlasting life."

The Law is the reflex of one side of the nature of Almighty God. The Law is the reflex of Almighty God's terrible holiness and His exact justice. The Law reveals what man is not. That is, *Man is not holy*--and the holy Law of Almighty God shows man just how unholy he is. Man is *not righteous*--and the righteous Law of God shows man exactly how unrighteous he really is. Natural man is not accepted before God. They that are in the flesh cannot please God. The natural man receiveth not the things of God, for they are spiritually discerned and he cannot know them, he cannot receive them. The Law reveals what the natural man really is. He is a sinner, he is vile, he is ungodly, he is hopeless, he is hopelessly lost, without God.

The Gospel of the marvelous grace of God is the Good News that the Law has been honored, the claims of the Law have been met. Jesus fulfilled every jot and every tittle of the holy Law, and satisfied Almighty God. The Good News is that Jesus honored the Law in every minute detail of His living; that He met the penalty of the Law in His sacrificial death. At the right hand of Almighty God, the risen man--the Man Christ Jesus-- is witness of God's eternal satisfaction concerning the finished work of His only begotten Son, who took a body that in the flesh He might do what the Law had never done (nor could ever have done in the flesh). The Gospel brings the Good News that there is forgiveness with God now, since Jesus satisfied the Law of God. The Gospel brings the Good News that life eternal can be ours if we will only accept the gift that God purchased in the death of Jesus, through the shed blood of His cross. The Gospel brings a new life . . . a new life in which and by which we may live above the Law--but only by faith, resting in the finished work of the Lord Jesus Christ. The Gospel brings new life, binding us to the heart of God in the vital union with His Son Jesus Christ, through the miracle of the new birth, which comes about through the incorruptible seed (The Word). If we accept the Son of God, and are born into the family of God, we will not stand before Him to be judged. We are heirs of God and joint-heirs with Jesus Christ through the miracle of the new birth.

The Gospel puts within our heart a new life, binding us to the heart of God in vital union with His Son, that we need no thunder of judgment to keep us right, and keep us in the straight and narrow way; but this new life so fills us with Christ that if we walk in the light as He is in the light, we have fellowship one with another . . . fellowship with the Son, and with the Father, and with the Spirit. We love one another as brethren and neighbors in the Lord even as we love ourselves. We love the God and Father of our Lord and Saviour, Jesus Christ, and we joy in God, who so loved us that He surrendered His only begotten Son that we might be saved through His shed blood.

The truest way to bring to God men who trust in the Law (so that His will may be righteously obeyed in their lives) is to preach to them the Gospel . . . the Good News of God's love; the Good News that Jesus fulfilled every jot and every tittle of the Law; the Good News that Christ is the end of the Law for righteousness to every one who believes; the Good News that ". . . what the Law could not do, in that it was weak through the flesh, God sending His own Son in the likeness of sinful flesh, and for sin, condemned sin in the flesh:" that we might become the righteousness of the Law in Jesus—but ONLY in Jesus. We need to preach the Love of God to these men. We will never be able to help those who are led about by divers doctrines by quarreling or fussing with them concerning their religion. Jesus said, "And I, if I be lifted up, I will draw all men unto me." He was signifying the death He would die; but if we will lift Him up in our daily living, in our testimony, in our walk and in our talk, we will prove to sinners and to deceived religionists that it is not commandments, rituals, or laws—but the gift of God—that saves and keeps men out of hell.

"By the deeds of the Law there shall no flesh be justified . . ." (Rom. 3:20). "Therefore, we conclude that a man is justified by faith without the deeds of the Law" (Rom. 3:28). "That no flesh should glory in His presence . . . Christ Jesus who of God is made unto us wisdom, and righteousness, and sanctification, and redemption; that, according as it is written, He that glorieth, let him glory in the Lord" (I Cor. 1:29–31).

O. B. G.

INTRODUCTION

Great Bible teachers of the past have called this epistle "Paul's Crucifixion Epistle," and "Paul's Explosive Epistle." One outstanding Bible teacher said, "Every sentence in it is a thunderbolt." Another great man of God said, "Every word in Galatians is a stick of dynamite." Martin Luther testified, "Galatians is my epistle. I am married to Galatians."

Certainly the book of Galatians was the pebble from the brook, with which (like David) Luther went forth to meet a giant . . . not a giant like unto David's Goliath, but a much more deadly giant—the *Papal* giant. Like David, Luther came out victorious. With the pebble of Galatians, he smote the Papal giant in the forehead!

Without a doubt, the epistle to the Galatians was used of God more than any other portion of the Bible, to bring about the Lutheran Reformation and the great stirring among the people of God.

Galatia was a Roman province. It included Antioch, Iconium, Lystra and Derbe, all of which cities were visited by Paul, and in them he ministered on his first great missionary journey. You will find the record in Acts 13 and 14. Please read these two chapters carefully. Time and space will not permit me to give you the text here.

In Acts 13:19 we have the account of the stoning of the Apostle Paul at Lystra. (There is strong evidence that Paul actually died . . . was stoned to death . . . and a great miracle was performed . . . he was raised from the dead.) But whether or not he was actually killed, a great miracle was performed. After Paul had been stoned and dragged outside of the city for dead, while his disciples stood round him mourning his death, "HE ROSE UP, AND CAME INTO THE CITY: AND THE NEXT

DAY HE DEPARTED WITH BARNABAS TO DERBE" (Acts 14:19-20).

Except for the miraculous power of Almighty God, it would have been impossible for a man to rise up and walk in such a short time after the stoning Paul received. Had it not been for the marvelous grace of God, Paul would not have gone immediately back into the city where he had been stoned, and from which he had just been dragged——supposedly a dead man!

Before Paul was stoned in the city of Lystra, he and Barnabas had actually been set up as gods, and the people worshipped them. Although the stoning was done by "certain Jews from Antioch and Iconium," the people in the city of Lystra were themselves persuaded to join these ungodly men in stoning Paul. However, the record tells us that Paul was permitted to remain in Lystra the night after the stoning, without further harm or disturbance. It is possible that the people were persuaded that there was something supernatural, something unusual, something extraordinary about this strange little man, Paul.

The city of Galatia was the home of the legend of Baucis and Philemon. According to the legend, the gods Jupiter and Mercury, traveling in disguise, visited Baucis and Philemon, and had given them the desires of their hearts. Paul and Barnabas came to Lystra, and God used them in the healing of the impotent man, "being a cripple from his mother's womb, who had never walked." The people supposed that the gods had come again to Lystra; therefore they lifted up their voices and cried out:

"The gods are come down to us in the likeness of men. And they called Barnabas, Jupiter; and Paul, Mercurius, because he was the chief speaker. Then the priest of Jupiter, which was before their city, brought oxen and garlands unto the gates, and would have done sacrifice with the people. Which when the apostles, Barnabas and Paul, heard of, they rent their clothes, and ran in among the people crying out, saying, Sirs, why do ye these things? We also are men of like passions with you, and preach unto you that ye should turn from these vanities unto the living God, which made heaven, and earth, and the sea, and all things that are therein: who in times past suffered all nations to walk in their own ways. Nevertheless He left not Himself without witness, in that He did good, and gave us rain from heaven, and fruitful seasons, filling our hearts with food and gladness. And with these sayings scarce restrained they the people, that they had not done sacrifice unto them" (Acts 14:8–18).

As I have already pointed out, it certainly did not take long (nor did it take very much) to turn these fickle, unstable, wishy-washy Galatians from an attitude of worship to one of hostility and brutal murder.

In Galatians 4:13 we read, "Ye know how through infirmity of the flesh I preached the gospel unto you at the first." This "infirmity of the flesh" may have been the result of Paul's experience at Lystra, which could have so disabled him that he was hindered from going on in his scheduled journeys and missionary endeavors; therefore, he preached the gospel to the Galatians instead. It could be that the stoning of Paul was a great blessing in disguise. It could be that this was God's way of giving to the church the marvelous book of Galatians.

Paul tells us in II Corinthians 12:1–10 that he knew a man (whether the man was in the body or out of the body he did not know) but such a man was caught up into the Third Heaven, into Paradise, and saw and heard things that were unlawful to tell. Since Bible authorities believe that II Corinthians was written about A. D. 60, it could be that Paul was referring to himself and his experience at Lystra when he was stoned and dragged outside the city for dead. He states "about fourteen years ago," and that would place the experience at the time of his stoning at Lystra. Personally, I believe he was referring to this experience; I believe Paul was dead; I believe they killed him, and his spirit ascended into Paradise. I believe the prayers of the saints, the faith of the saints, brought Paul's spirit back to his body, and he was literally raised from the dead!

In this marvelous testimony in II Corinthians 12:1–10, Paul speaks of a "third heaven, Paradise," and of the wonderful revelations he received there——revelations which were unlawful to make known. He said, "Lest I should be exalted above measure . . . there was given to me a thorn in the flesh." He prayed three times that this thorn in the flesh might be removed, but God did not see fit to answer his prayer; but He assured Paul, "My grace is sufficient for thee: for my strength is made perfect in weakness." Paul responded to this wonderful revelation by saying, "Most gladly therefore will I rather glory in my infirmities, that the power of Christ may rest upon me. Therefore I take pleasure in infirmities, in reproaches, in necessities, in persecutions, in distresses for Christ's sake: for when I am weak, then am I strong" (II Cor. 12:7–10).

Regardless of where Paul preached, he had one message: "Jesus Christ——crucified, buried, risen, coming again!" He preached the Gospel to the Galatians. He went throughout the province of Galatia, preaching the Gospel of the marvelous grace of God . . . salvation by grace, through faith, plus nothing! Many believed and were saved. Later, Paul addressed these believers as "the churches of Galatia," referring to the local assemblies which had been organized by the believers in the province of Galatia. However, false teachers followed Paul, preaching a double error, double heresy, and because of this Paul wrote the epistle to the Galatians.

These false teachers preached that the way of salvation for the sinner is partly by faith in the grace of God, and partly by works and obedience to the Law of Moses. In the second place, these false teachers taught that the way a saved person is kept saved and finally perfected in the Lord and glorified, is by means of his own good works, good living, and obedience to the Law of Moses. That is, they preached that we are *saved* by grace, but *keep* our salvation by keeping the Law of Moses. Thus, the double error.

Paul answered these false teachers by proving salvation is by grace, through faith in the finished work of the Lamb of God—*plus nothing*. He showed to the Galatians that salvation had been going on for hundreds of years before Moses was born, before the Law of Moses ever came into existence. Paul preached that the way of salvation was then as it is now—as it always has been and always will be: through faith alone, apart from works or the keeping of the Law. "Therefore by the deeds of the law there shall no flesh be justified . . ." (Romans 3:20a).

In Galatians, Paul shows that the Law of Moses has no part in keeping a believer saved; nor does the Law of Moses have any part in the believer's final perfection and glorification. A saved person is kept saved by the "power of God" who dwells within us, and not by anything he or she may do. The Holy Ghost of God, the Third Person of the Trinity, abides in the bosom of every believer. He draws us to Christ, He "borns" us into the body of Christ, He seals us until the day of redemption, He leads us in paths of right living——and in the sweet bye-and-bye He will quicken our mortal bodies and we will have a glorious body like unto the body of the Lord Jesus after His resurrection. To the Galatians, Paul preached that it is God who saves us, that it is God who keeps us——and that God alone *can* keep us. "Wherefore let him that thinketh he standeth take heed lest he fall" (I Cor. 10:12).

While all Scripture is inspired and is profitable to us (II Timothy 3:16) it would be utterly impossible for me to overemphasize the importance of the epistle to the Galatians. This epistle was probably written A. D. 60, during the third visit of Paul to the city of Corinth. It had come to Paul's knowledge that Galatians who were not Greeks, but who were Gauls——"a stream from the torrent of barbarians which poured into Greece in the third century before Christ"——had become prey of the Jewish legalizers. These Judaizing missionaries from Palestine were the false teachers who preached a mixture of Law and Grace for salvation——and for the *keeping* of salvation.

According to Dr. Scofield, the theme of Galatians is "the vindication of the Gospel of the grace of God from any admixture of law-conditions, which qualify or destroy its character of pure grace." (If you do not have a Scofield study Bible, please do not let another day pass without your purchasing a Scofield Reference Bible.)

CONTENTS

	Preface	iii
	Introduction	vii
I.	Paul's Authority as an Apostle Chapter 1:1–5	15
II.	Occasion and Theme of Galatians Chapter 1:6–9	28
III.	Paul's Message Was from God—Not Men Chapter 1:10–2:14	33
IV.	Justification by Faith Without Law—Works Chapter 2:15–21	58
V.	The Gift of the Spirit Comes by Faith— Not by Law or by Works Chapter 3:1–12	72
VI.	Christ Has Borne for Us the Curse of the Law— That We Might Have the Blessing of Faith Chapter 3:13–14	87
VII.	The Abrahamic and the Mosaic Covenants Chapter 3:15–4:10	94
VIII.	The Departed Blessing Chapter 4:11–5:15	120
IX.	Victory Over Sin Comes through the Holy Spirit Chapter 5:16–6:18	157

THE EPISTLE OF PAUL THE APOSTLE TO THE GALATIANS

CHAPTER ONE

1. Paul, an apostle, (not of men, neither by man, but by Jesus Christ, and God the Father, who raised him from the dead;)

2. And all the brethren which are with me, unto the churches of Galatia:

3. Grace be to you and peace from God the Father, and from our Lord Jesus Christ,

4. Who gave himself for our sins, that he might deliver us from this present evil world, according to the will of God and our Father:

5. To whom be glory for ever and ever. Amen.

6. I marvel that ye are so soon removed from him that called you into the grace of Christ unto another gospel:

7. Which is not another; but there be some that trouble you, and would pervert the gospel of Christ.

8. But though we, or an angel from heaven, preach any other gospel unto you than that which we have preached unto you, let him be accursed.

9. As we said before, so say I now again, If any man preach any other gospel unto you than that ye have received, let him be accursed.

10. For do I now persuade men, or God? or do I seek to please men? for if I yet pleased men, I should not be the servant of Christ.

11. But I certify you, brethren, that the gospel which was preached of me is not after man.

12. For I neither received it of man, neither was I taught it, but by the revelation of Jesus Christ.

13. For ye have heard of my conversation in time past in the Jews' religion, how that beyond measure I persecuted the church of God, and wasted it:

14. And profited in the Jews' religion above many my equals in mine own nation, being more exceedingly zealous of the traditions of my fathers.

15. But when it pleased God, who separated me from my mother's womb, and called me by his grace,

16. To reveal his Son in me, that I might preach him among the heathen; immediately I conferred not with flesh and blood:

17. Neither went I up to Jerusalem to them which were apostles before me; but I went into Arabia, and returned again unto Damascus.

18. Then after three years I went up to Jerusalem to see Peter, and abode with him fifteen days.

19. But other of the apostles saw I none, save James the Lord's brother.

20. Now the things which I write unto you, behold, before God, I lie not.

21. Afterwards I came into the regions of Syria and Cilicia;

22. And was unknown by face unto the churches of Judaea which were in Christ:

23. But they had heard only, That he which persecuted us in times past now preacheth the faith which once he destroyed.

24. And they glorified God in me.

PAUL'S AUTHORITY AS AN APOSTLE

We find Paul's apostolic greeting in chapter 1, verses 1 through 5: "Paul, an apostle, (not of men, neither by man, but by Jesus Christ, and God the Father, who raised Him from the dead)."

There is something unusual in this beginning of Paul's greeting to the Galatians. You will note his introduction does not follow the custom of his introduction to other epistles . . . that is, the custom of "giving thanks." Notice the first verses of the other epistles of Paul, and you will see in almost every one of them that he begins by thanking God for the believers in that particular city or area. But how could he give thanks for these Galatians who were turning from the grace of God, and returning to dead legalism? I thank God for the statement made in verse 1: "An apostle (not of men, neither BY man, BUT BY JESUS CHRIST AND GOD THE FATHER, who raised Him from the dead!" I do not judge when I make this statement: I am afraid we have too many apostles today (ministers, preachers, evangelists, Bible teachers) who ARE apostles of men, called by men, sent by men, and their message is to please men. I am afraid we have too many "assembly line" preachers today. You and I know that if a young man does not attend the denominational school or the denominational seminary, he does not have much of a chance at a big church in his particular denomination. The big denominations of our day are turning ministers off the assembly line like the automobile manufacturers turn automobiles off the assembly line. I am afraid that is the reason we have "a famine in the land" . . . not a famine of bread, not a famine of water, not a famine of crowds, big churches and big programs with bushel baskets of money——but a famine of the preaching of the Word, a famine of the hearing of the Word, because many of our ministers and pastors today are sent by the denomination they represent, rather than being sent by Almighty God.

Paul wanted it clearly understood that he was God's apostle, sent by God and the Lord Jesus Christ, and not of men.

Paul wanted it clearly understood that he did not receive his apostleship from those who were apostles before him. Later, he proved this fact. He also proved that his commission came from the nail-pierced hand of the risen Christ, and from God the Father who sent the Son to die for the sin of the world and raised Him from the dead for our justification. Paul left no stone unturned to make it clear that he was God's preacher, and that his ministry was not for sale.

Paul's message was a new message . . . a mystery not known before. His message, received direct from heaven, was a new revelation of divine truth. The heart of Paul's message was "the grace of God," and that the grace of God had been extended to all men everywhere regardless of nationality——Jew or Gentile, Greeks or Barbarians——Jesus Christ died for all, and invites all . . . "whosoever *will*," let him come.

The message before the grace of God had been limited to the nation Israel, and the Gentiles could be saved only by becoming Jews, by submitting to the Jewish rite of circumcision, thus placing themselves under the laws and the rituals of the Israelites. These were called "Jewish proselytes." When Paul came with this new message of salvation by grace through faith plus nothing, he met with serious opposition from the eleven apostles who were preaching the Kingdom message to the Jews only. Paul was a Jew . . . he was born in Tarsus. He was the son of a Roman citizen. He received his education in Tarsus, and received his theological training in the seminary in Jerusalem, under the teaching of the great Gamaliel (Acts 22:3). Paul was a member of the Sanhedrin, the highest ruling religious body in Israel. He was a very prominent member of the strictest sect of the Pharisees (Acts 26:5). I trust you will read the entire twenty-sixth chapter of Acts.

Paul was devoted to Judaism, soul, spirit and body. He was a fanatic in his defense of what he believed to be the only true religion on earth. Paul was present when Stephen was martyred. He became the most bitter enemy Christianity had in his day. He was traveling to Damascus to arrest Christians and persecute the church when he was struck down and blinded by a light from heaven. He called out, asking who it was speaking to him. The answer recorded in Acts 9:5 was: "I am Jesus whom thou persecutest." Through this gigantic experience, Paul became a believer, was baptized, and preached Jesus in the synagogues.

After his conversion he visited Jerusalem, but the believers there were afraid of him because they knew him as an enemy of the church. He soon left Jerusalem and went to his home city of Tarsus. From Tarsus he went into Arabia where he spent three years. It was in Arabia that he received the revelation of this new message . . . the mystery of the church, the body of Christ, the age of grace . . . salvation by grace through faith plus nothing.

After spending three years in Arabia, Paul returned

to Tarsus where Barnabas joined him. They went to Antioch, where they labored for twelve months. A great number of Gentiles were converted and became believers through the ministry of Paul and Barnabas.

After the year of ministry in Antioch, Paul and Barnabas made a trip to Jerusalem to bring gifts for relief of the poor suffering Jewish disciples in Jerusalem. When they returned to Antioch, they were sent forth as the first Christian missionaries. The rest of the book of *The Acts of the Apostles* deals almost entirely with the journeys and the ministry of the Apostle Paul.

After Paul's first missionary journey, he was called upon to give a report concerning his message to the Gentiles, and their conversion. Read the entire fifteenth chapter of Acts carefully, and you will learn much concerning salvation by grace for "whosoever will." Of course the enemies of Paul accused him of preaching heresy. They went to Jerusalem and made a report to the apostles there. During this conference it was decided that the message of grace which Paul preached was truly the message of Christ from Heaven. It was decided that the Gentile believers were not under Jewish law, nor under Jewish rituals. It is interesting to note that this is the last time the apostles in the Holy City of Jerusalem are mentioned. Peter and the rest of the apostles preaching the Kingdom message to Israel, bow out of the picture because Israel as a nation is temporarily set aside, the Kingdom has been temporarily postponed until the fulness of the Gentiles comes in, the grace of God is preached, the church is completed and caught up to meet Jesus in the air. Then, after the anti-Christ has his reign, the Gospel of the Kingdom will be preached again and all Israel will be saved (Romans, chapter 11).

Notice the sharp and distinct difference between the

message of the Apostle Paul and the messages of the other apostles. Peter's message was to Israel . . . Paul's message was to the Gentiles. He was called and commissioned a minister to the Gentiles (Rom. 11:13). ". . . When they saw that the gospel of the uncircumcision was committed unto me (Paul) as the gospel of the circumcision was unto Peter . . ." (Gal. 2:7).

The apostles, as well as the seventy, were commanded to go to the Jews only. They preached the message of the Kingdom. Only one time did any one of the apostles preach to a Gentile. This instance was when Peter preached at the house of Cornelius (Acts 10). This was the time Peter used the keys of the Kingdom in presenting the Gospel to the Gentiles for the very first time. The apostles established no churches outside of Judaea. They limited their ministry to Jerusalem, and to the lost sheep of the house of Israel. After the stoning of Stephen, the church was scattered everywhere. The apostles continued in Jerusalem, ministering only to Israel. After Stephen's death, we read, "They were all scattered abroad throughout the regions of Judaea and Samaria, EXCEPT THE APOSTLES" (Acts 8:1). Please note again: "They which were scattered abroad upon the persecution that arose about Stephen travelled as far as Phenice, and Cyprus, and Antioch, preaching the word to none but unto the Jews only" (Acts 11:19).

The apostles never founded any Gentile churches. Paul (God's messenger for this dispensation with the message of Grace) was the man who founded Gentile assemblies . . . churches in Antioch, Corinth, Galatia, Thessalonica, Ephesus, Philippi, Colosse, and many others. If we do not keep in mind that Paul's message was to all men regardless of class or color, we cannot rightly divide the word of truth and reconcile the message of the Apostle Paul with the message of the other apostles.

During the days the apostles and the seventy preached (commissioned by the Lord Jesus), Gentiles were known as unclean dogs outside the covenant of grace. When Paul began to preach to the Gentiles the message of salvation by grace alone through faith in the shed blood of Jesus, bitter opposition arose and Paul suffered much for preaching salvation by grace through faith plus nothing. The apostles refused to accept Paul as an apostle because he did not receive his commission from them in Jerusalem, and he did not preach the same apostolic message they preached. Therefore, they rejected him as an apostle.

Notice briefly the difference between the Kingdom message and the message given to the Apostle Paul: In Matthew 10 we have the Kingdom message preached by the apostles: "And when He had called unto Him His twelve disciples, He gave them power against unclean spirits, to cast them out, and to heal all manner of sickness and all manner of disease" (Matt. 10:1).

Notice this solemn fact: "These twelve Jesus sent forth, and commanded them, saying, Go not into the way of the Gentiles, and into any city of the Samaritans enter ye not: but go rather to the lost sheep of the house of Israel" (Matt. 10:5–6).

The message of the apostles was not the message for the church, but for Israel alone. The message announced "the Kingdom of Heaven is at hand." The message offered the setting up of the Messianic kingdom upon the condition of national repentance in Israel. *Paul's* message was: "BELIEVE ON THE LORD JESUS CHRIST AND THOU SHALT BE SAVED" (Acts 16:31).

Signs and wonders were evidences of the Kingdom message given to the apostles: "Heal the sick, cleanse the lepers, raise the dead, cast out devils: freely ye have received, freely give" (Matt. 10:8).

For ministers today to use this verse as authority for healing the sick, and then to ignore the rest of the Scripture, is certainly to wrongly divide the Word of God, not "rightly dividing the word of truth." The apostles not only healed *"all manner of sickness,"* but they also RAISED THE DEAD AND CLEANSED THE LEPERS! I believe in divine healing . . . if there IS any healing, it is divine. God heals our bodies when we are sick. Thank God for doctors, thank God for nurses and hospitals; but when all doctors fail, God is able to intervene. Nevertheless, it is wrong to use the Kingdom commission to declare that all ministers today should have the gift of healing, should be able to raise the dead and cast out demons. We should never wrongly divide the Word of God and misapply Scripture to prove a religious point. We should face the Bible fact of dispensational truth. The message of the apostles was sanctioned by signs and wonders, but in this marvelous day of grace, "the just shall live by faith" (Rom. 1:17).

There is another interesting thing about the apostles: "Provide neither gold, nor silver, nor brass in your purses, nor scrip for your journey, neither two coats, neither shoes, nor yet staves: for the workman is worthy of his meat" (Matt. 10:9—10).

Certainly that does not sound like modern day ministers and evangelists, does it? Do ministers today refuse gold and silver in their purses, scrip for their journey? Do ministers today refuse two coats, and do they refuse the many things showered upon them by their parishioners? The apostles were a specific group with a singular message to a peculiar people chosen of God—— *the nation Israel.*

Many today use the first part of Matthew 10 for their

advantage . . . "Heal the sick," but they do not notice the part "Provide neither gold, silver, nor brass in your purses." I believe we should be consistent in our preaching, consistent in our living, and consistent in our religious practices.

Suppose we compare the apostolic message of the Kingdom with the message of grace given to the Apostle Paul:

The commission today is "Go ye into all the world and preach the Gospel to every creature." But to the apostles the commission was, "Go NOT into the way of the Gentiles; go only to the lost sheep of the house of Israel."

Notice these words: "For there is no difference between the Jew and the Greek: for the same Lord over all is rich unto all that call upon Him. For whosoever shall call upon the name of the Lord shall be saved" (Rom. 10:12–13). How can this message be reconciled with the message "Go not to the Gentiles"? The only way to understand the Word of God is to study and rightly divide the word of truth. Paul's message was concerning "the dispensation of grace." We MUST face dispensational truth, or we cannot understand the Word of God.

Someone may be asking, "Brother Greene, did God change His mind?" NO! "Has God's law been destroyed?" NO! But beloved, God commanded the adulterers and adulteresses to be stoned under the Law of Moses; but *Jesus* dealt in mercy with one who was taken in the very act of adultery! The Law commands a rebellious child to be stoned (Deut. 21:18–21), but the father tenderly took the prodigal in his arms and kissed him--hogpen clothes and all! (Luke 15:11–24). Under the Law of Moses, a thief was condemned (Exodus 21:16), but on the cross, in His last moments, Jesus saved a thief (Luke

23:43). The Law cries out, "An eye for an eye, a tooth for a tooth, a hand for a hand and a foot for a foot!" (Exodus 21:24); but the grace of God preached by Paul thunders out, "IF THINE ENEMY HUNGER, FEED HIM; IF HE THIRST, GIVE HIM DRINK" (Rom. 12:20). It is absolutely impossible to reconcile such Scriptures, unless we recognize dispensational truth in the Word of God. During the Dispensation of Law, God dealt with Israel in a specific way; but in this *Dispensation of Grace,* there is no such thing as Jew and Gentile. The Lord Jesus Christ is rich in mercy unto all that call upon Him. The Law condemns the sinner . . . but the Grace of God forgives the sinner and justifies the ungodly in the sight of a holy God.

Do not think that God has done away with Israel . . . oh, no! Israel is set aside as a chosen nation, but one day God will turn again to His people and they will receive their Messiah. They will see the scars in His hands, they will accept Him, and all Israel will be saved. (Read the entire eleventh chapter of Romans.)

Paul's severe persecution was the result of the failure of the people of his day to recognize the difference between Law and Grace . . . the difference between the Dispensation of Law and the Dispensation of Grace. Certainly people have not changed today. Failure on the part of most church members to study the Bible, to face it as a book of dispensational truth, is still causing much misunderstanding among believers and much division in local assemblies. I am sure that ninety-five percent of all the difficulty in local churches would end, if church members (believers) would recognize the difference between Law and Grace, and if they would recognize God's program for national Israel and God's plan for the church (the Bride of Christ). To apply to the church the promises God made to Israel can only lead to religious confusion and misunderstanding. It was for the purpose of correcting this error in the church that Paul wrote the letter to the Galatians. We need it today just as badly as they needed it then. My earnest prayer as I send out this message, is that you, dear reader, will recognize that God saves us by grace through faith plus nothing. We are kept by the power of God because of the grace of God in allowing the Lord Jesus to take our place and become accursed for us. Through Him we are "more than conquerors" . . . but only through the Lord Jesus Christ (Rom. 8:35–39). "Wherefore let him that thinketh he standeth take heed lest he fall" (Rom. 10:12). Thank God, we are more than conquerors through the Lord Jesus Christ. What the Law could not do in that it was weak through the flesh, God sent His only begotten Son into the world in the likeness of sinful flesh, and for sin condemned sin in the flesh that you and I might become the righteousness of God in Jesus. He who knew no sin was made sin for us, that we in Jesus might become righteous (II Cor. 5:21).

Galatians 1:2: "And all the brethren which are with me, unto the churches of Galatia." Exactly who these brethren were, we cannot tell, because we do not know for sure whether this epistle was written at Ephesus or at Corinth. Some outstanding Bible authorities believe it was written at Ephesus, others believe it to have been written at Corinth, but this is unimportant. The important thing is that Paul speaks with the authority of an apostle, and with the full authority of the Father and of the Son he writes as he is moved by the Holy Ghost. His message to the Galatians was from Almighty God—— not from man.

Paul's statement "unto the churches" refers, of course, to believers throughout Galatia. They probably met in homes, or in halls. Again——where they met is not important. Stained glass windows and carpets on the floors will not make a church. A building with a magnificent steeple does not make a church. It will be a happy day in the lives of some believers when they recognize the *building* as the meeting place of the church, and not the church itself. The New Testament church is a group of born again believers, fellowshipping and worshipping together in the name of the Lord; and certainly God puts His stamp of approval on the local assembly (Heb. 10:25).

Galatians 1:3: "Grace be to you and peace from God the Father, and from our Lord Jesus Christ." To us, that statement is not outstanding. We hear the word "grace" every time we attend church. (If you do not hear it, you should change your place of worship!) But imagine how it must have sounded to those in Galatia who had become believers, who had been rescued from heathenism and idolatry! It was by the grace of God that peace had come into their lives, and the peace they enjoyed was made possible through the shed blood of the Lord Jesus Christ. Paul clearly states to the Colossians that Jesus "made peace through the blood of His cross." May God help you and me to not overlook the sacrifice of Calvary when God delivered up His Son to pay the sin-debt with His own precious blood! Never forget, beloved, that God Almighty purchased the New Testament church at a tremendous price:

"Take heed therefore unto yourselves, and to all the flock, over the which the Holy Ghost hath made you overseers, *to feed the church of God which He (God)* HATH PURCHASED WITH HIS OWN BLOOD" (Acts 20:28). Weigh this statement before you criticize it. It is a Bible fact. You may not accept it, but it is the truth: In the veins of the Lord Jesus Christ ran the blood of Jehovah God! Jesus took part of humanity . . . He took flesh from the Virgin Mary; but His blood was the blood of Jehovah

God. God purchased the New Testament church, the Bride of Christ, with His own blood. What a price! No wonder Paul was jealous for the Gospel of Grace!

Verses 4 and 5: "Who gave Himself for our sins, that He might deliver us from this present evil world, according to the will of God and our Father: To whom be glory forever and ever. Amen."

In John chapter 10, Jesus testified to His people that God the Father loved Him because He laid His life down for the sheep. He declared that no man could *take* His life——He had the power to lay it down, He had the power to take it again (John 10:18); and then He preached that "This commandment received I from my Father." God the Father, God the Son, and God the Holy Ghost provided our redemption. God the Father so loved the world, that He gave God the Son to die on the cross. God the Son willingly laid down His life for the ungodly, and conquered death, hell and the grave. After His resurrection He showed Himself openly by many infallible proofs. Five hundred brethren saw Him at one time (I Cor. 15:1–10). Jesus, having finished His mission on earth, said, "Nevertheless I tell you the truth; It is expedient for you that I go away: for if I go not away, the Comforter will not come unto you; but if I depart, I will send Him unto you. And when He is come, He will reprove the world of sin, and of righteousness, and of judgment: Of sin, because they believe not on me; Of righteousness, because I go to my Father, and ye see me no more; Of judgment, because the prince of this world is judged" (John 16:7–11).

Jesus ascended back to the Father, and on the day of Pentecost the Holy Ghost came. He has been in the world since that day, convicting men of sin, drawing men to Jesus, "borning" men into the family of God when they put their faith in the finished work of the Lord Jesus Christ. "Not by works of righteousness which we have done, but according to His mercy He saved us, by the washing of regeneration, and renewing of the Holy Ghost" (Titus 3:5). Because our sins were so thoroughly dealt with, so completely paid for and so righteously disposed of, grace and peace are our possessions when we possess the Lord Jesus by faith.

The reason God permitted His Son to suffer such agony of soul, spirit and body . . . the reason God permitted Him to become a curse for you and for me . . . the reason God permitted Him to die for the ungodly was that through the death of Jesus we might be delivered from this present evil age and made fit for the kingdom of God. Surely, we who are believers can happily and heartily join in the Doxology here written by Paul: "TO HIM BE GLORY FOREVER AND EVER. AMEN!"

If I had ten thousand hands, I would raise them all for Jesus! If I had a voice like the thunders of the heavens I would thunder out, "Thank God for Jesus!" If I could speak to the whole wide world at one time, I would be compelled to incorporate in my message the words, "Thanks be unto God for His unspeakable gift!"

Let me sum up the message of these verses: First of all, *the channel of God's grace* is the Lord Jesus Christ who gave Himself willingly on the cross, for our sins. He died for our sins "according to the Scriptures."

In the second place, *the purpose of the grace of God* is to deliver us . . . poor, lost, hell-deserving sinners . . . from this present evil world. "The whole world lieth in the lap of the wicked one," and were it not for God's grace we would all be lost eternally.

In the third place, *the source of God's grace* is the

sovereign will and purpose of Jehovah God: "According to the will of God and our Father."

According to Hebrews 2:9 it was only because of the grace of God that Jesus was permitted to take a body in which He could die. We must face the fact that Jesus was God in flesh (II Cor. 5:19). Jesus wrapped God up in flesh and brought Him down to man. It was by the grace of God that Jesus was permitted to die; therefore, the source of grace is the sovereign God.

In the fourth place, *the reason for God's grace* is to bring glory and honor to God the Father (and to God only) for ever and forever. Never forget that God saves us for Jesus' sake (Eph. 4:30–32).

It is humanly impossible to define the grace of God. It is humanly impossible to *understand* the grace of God; but thanks be unto God, it is NOT humanly impossible to ACCEPT the grace of God! Grace is God's gift—and even a child knows how to come into possession of a gift: Simply receive it (with thanksgiving) from the giver. Therefore, the message of grace is, "As many as received Him, to them gave He power to become the sons of God, even to them that believe on His name: which were born . . . born of God" (John 1:12–13).

The occasion and the theme of Galatians:

Verse 6: "I marvel that ye are so soon removed from Him that called you into the grace of Christ unto another gospel."

Paul was amazed, he was astonished, he marveled that anyone who had received the grace of God could ever entertain the idea of departing from the marvelous grace of God, with the liberty of soul and spirit that grace brings. Paul marveled that anyone who had really known the Gospel of the grace of God should turn from it. Paul had been a religionist––a devout Judaist. He was a fanatic in the religion of the Jews. Paul was an educated man; he had studied the Law of Moses from A to Z, and from Z back to A. He was not a religious dumb-cluck nor an ignoramus. To Paul, the discovery of the grace of God was so wonderful and so marvelous, that he was astonished beyond measure that anyone could come into the possession of the peace and joy that grace brings, and then turn again to the rituals of the Law! And yet–– it seemed that the believers at Galatia were removing from the grace that he had preached unto them, through which they had been so gloriously saved.

Paul mentions "unto another gospel . . . which is *not* another." That is, they were removing from the pure Gospel of the grace of God, to another message (another gospel) that was not really Gospel. The Gospel is the Good News, and any other message than the true one could not be a gospel at all.

In one of the outstanding commentaries, we read that at the time of Paul, the Galatians had written more than seventy gospels! Of course they were not genuine–– they were not true Gospels. They had either added to or subtracted from the message of Paul, and it was to these gospels (which were really not Good News) that the Galatians were turning.

Verse 7: ". . . Which is not another; but there be some that trouble you, and would pervert the Gospel of Christ." We know Satan is on the job. Jesus said when the tares were sown among the wheat, "An enemy hath done this." That same enemy is still in the business of sowing tares. Satan has many evil spirits and emissaries in the world today. The very air we breathe is filled with demons. The kingdom of Satan is just above us––

and he hates the Gospel of the grace of God. In writing to the church at Corinth Paul said, ". . . Such are false apostles, deceitful workers, transforming themselves into the apostles of Christ. And no marvel; for Satan himself is transformed into an angel of light. Therefore it is no great thing if his ministers also be transformed as the ministers of righteousness; whose end shall be according to their works" (II Cor. 11:13-15).

Never forget that just as surely as God has churches and ministers, the devil also has churches and ministers. God calls evangelists—and the *devil* calls evangelists; God calls Sunday school teachers—and the *devil* calls Sunday school teachers. The devil has a cheap counterfeit for every genuine product of spirituality and the true church. In Galatia, the emissaries of the devil were preaching another gospel—which was not a gospel at all.

Verse 8: "But though we, or an angel from heaven, preach any other gospel unto you than that which we have preached unto you, let him be accursed." That does not sound like some of the lovely preaching we hear today, does it, beloved? That is . . . that "we are all brothers," the "fatherhood of God, the brotherhood of man" . . . we are supposed to love and fellowship with the liberals, the modernists and the haters of God . . . those who deny the virgin birth and those who would destroy our Bible by leaving out words like "Jehovah," "blood," "virgin," "new birth," etc. Certainly the words of Paul do not sound like the words of some of the seminary-trained denominational preachers of our day. So Paul thunders out, "Even though it be we (Paul and Barnabas) or an angel from *Heaven* . . . if we or an angel or anyone else preach any gospel except the Gospel we have already preached unto you, *let him be accursed.*" That means, "Let that person (or that angel) drop into hellfire!" It would be difficult to find anything from Genesis to Revelation more dreadful than that statement. The devil may transform himself into an angel of light, and his ministers may transform themselves as the ministers of righteousness; but whether it BE an angel from heaven, or one of the devil's emissaries transformed as an angel . . . or even if it be Paul himself . . . if that person preaches any other gospel than the Gospel of the Grace of God which Paul had already preached to the Galatian Christians, Paul said, "Let that preacher drop into hell . . . let that preacher be accursed! Do not let him deliver any message except the message of the grace of God!"

In Galatians 5:12, Paul thunders out, "I would they were even cut off which trouble you!" That statement would not go over so well, either, in one of the meetings of the National Council of Churches of Christ in America ——or The World Council of Churches, where birds of a feather flock together and demand that all ministers come under their wings. God have mercy on any two-legged human being who claims to be called of God, who claims to be a minister of God . . . and yet will support atheism and liberalism such as is in these councils of churches around the world!

No, I do not believe the Apostle Paul would be invited to join the average ministerial association . . . and frankly, I do not think he would be invited to join some of the "fellowships" across the country. This man preached because preach he MUST. He was called of God, ordained of God, sent by God——and he must give an account TO God; therefore, he preached pure Gospel.

Verse 9: "As we said before, so say I now again, If any man preach any other gospel unto you than that ye have received, let him be accursed." Paul wanted the Galatians to fully understand what he was saying. He laid double emphasis upon the apostolic anathema which he pronounced upon all preachers of a gospel that is not the Gospel of the Grace of God. God help you and me to remind ourselves that the message has not changed—neither has the curse been withdrawn. Even today, according to the Bible, any person is accursed who preaches any gospel except the pure Gospel of the marvelous grace of God. In Galatia the false teachers were teaching that believers could not be saved by faith alone—but must add their own good works in obedience to the Law of Moses. Furthermore, they were teaching that a believer could not be *kept* saved except by works and obedience to the same Law of Moses. We should look around us and listen to some of the preaching today. If we will stop, look, and listen, we will recognize the Galatian heresy in this day. Many preachers preach salvation by grace, through faith, *plus works*. Oh, they scream out, "Grace, grace . . . God's grace . . . grace that is greater than all our sin . . ." but then in the next breath they command their parishioners to practice certain "do's" and "dont's," and if they do not practice these religious and denominational "do's" and "dont's" they will surely be damned! But according to the Apostle Paul, "It is not by works of righteousness which we have done, but according to His mercy . . . He saves us by the washing of regeneration and the renewing of the Holy Ghost."

God help us to see the difference between *redemption* and *reward* . . . *salvation* and *stewardship*. Salvation is God's gift to a hell-deserving sinner. Believers are rewarded for their faithful stewardship. Read I Corinthians 3:11–15. In these verses, Paul clearly points out that some believers will lose their reward. Salvation is a gift totally and entirely of God . . . totally and entirely apart from works. The sinner cannot do anything to save himself or to help God save him. The sinner receives Jesus by faith, and the grace of God saves his soul.

When the sinner believes and becomes a Christian —then the *reward* at the end of the Christian life will be determined by faithful works. Salvation is not of works —but *salvation works*. Salvation makes us want to work. We ARE His workmanship, created in Christ Jesus unto good works——and faith without works is dead. Works testify that we have exercised saving faith in the grace of God——and the person who refuses to bring forth fruit certainly testifies that his faith is dead faith . . . and dead faith cannot save the sinner.

God pity some of the preachers of our day, when they stand before God Almighty to receive their reward. God pity the preacher who supplements the Gospel of Grace with the gospel of works! God pity the preacher who puts the denomination ahead of the grace of God . . . the program of the local church ahead of the grace of God. As ministers of the Gospel, we are commanded to lift up the Lord Jesus Christ, to preach the grace of God, to declare the whole counsel of God, and to study, rightly dividing the word of truth. God pity the minister who wrongly handles God's truth!

PAUL'S MESSAGE WAS A REVEALED MESSAGE FROM GOD——NOT A MESSAGE RECEIVED FROM OTHER APOSTLES.

Verse 10: "For do I now persuade men, or God? Or do I seek to please men? For if I yet pleased men, I should not be the servant of Christ."

What Paul is saying in this verse is simply this: "Am I seeking to please men? or God? Am I seeking the favor of men, or the favor of God? If I were pleasing men, then I could not please God——and therefore I could not be a servant of Christ." (The Greek word used here for "servant" is actually "bond-servant" or "bond-slave.") Paul knew that since the Lord Jesus Christ was his Lord and leader, he had become a slave to Christ . . . and he gloried in the fact that he was a bond-servant of Jesus Christ. He used the title with the right kind of pride: ". . . the slave of Jesus Christ" (Rom. 1:1). A slave has only one person to please, and that person is his lord and master. The slave has but one thing to do——and that is the will of his master. The enemies of Paul said that he sought the favor of men, that he sought to *please* men. Paul replied, "I am seeking only the favor of my Lord, and if I were striving to please men ——even if I succeeded in pleasing them——while striving for their favor I could not be the slave of Christ."

What was true concerning Paul is also true concerning us. We should settle the question, *"Who is our Lord?"* Whose slave are we? As believers, who are we trying to please? Whose favor are we seeking? Are we seeking the favor of men——or the favor of God? *If we please God we cannot please man.* Jesus Christ never satisfied *all* of the people——some praised Him, while others blasphemed. Some honored Him while others dishonored Him with words of slander. The same is true today . . . the minister who preaches the true Gospel will be appreciated by some, and hated by many! Whose bond-servant are *you*? Whose bond-servant . . . whose minister . . . am *I*?

Verses 11 and 12: "But I certify you, brethren, that the Gospel which was preached to me is not after man. For I neither received it of man, neither was I taught it, but by the revelation of Jesus Christ."

Here Paul is stating again what he had already said in verse 1, declaring that the Gospel is not from man nor from any human source, but by revelation of the Lord Jesus Christ. Paul did not visit the apostles at Jerusalem and ask them what to preach, what message to deliver

. . . what tradition to follow; nor did he ask them to give to him the apostolic commission (or authority) to minister. He did not go to a denominational theological seminary to gain his knowledge from the esteemed faculty of such an institution. Paul was not ordained by man or by the laying on of human hands; he was ordained of God. There were three years between his glorious conversion on the road to Damascus and the beginning of his public ministry as an apostle to the Gentiles. During these three years he received instructions from the risen Christ.

There are twenty-seven books in the New Testament —thirteen of them begin with the same word: *"Paul."* If we accept Paul as the author of Hebrews, there are fourteen of the twenty-seven books written by the apostle to the Gentiles. Matthew wrote one book, Mark wrote one, Luke wrote two, John wrote five, and Peter wrote two. Jude and James each wrote one book. The other apostles did not write any of the Epistles. Mark and Luke were not among the twelve apostles, and received much of their information from the Apostle Paul. Luke wrote the book of Acts, and over half of that book is given over to the account of Paul's conversion, experiences, and missionary journeys. Seventeen chapters of Acts deal with the life of Paul. After the fifteenth chapter of Acts, the other apostles are not mentioned. Their ministry to Israel disappears in the light of Paul's ministry, ordained of God to the Gentiles.

Because Paul's message was new and unique in every aspect—a different message from that delivered by the original apostles—it was not readily accepted by them. His message was a direct revelation from heaven. He was vigorously opposed by the legalizers and by the legalistic teachers of his day. They followed him from city to city, attempting to discredit the authority of his message of salvation by grace through faith plus nothing.

As a result, Paul was time and again called upon to come to the defense of himself against his accusers, and to prove his divine authority to speak as an apostle. In reading the epistles dictated to Paul by the Holy Ghost, you will note the following:

The epistle to the Romans opens, "Paul, a servant of Jesus Christ, called to be an apostle."

The first epistle to the Corinthians opens with, "Paul, called to be an apostle of Jesus Christ through the will of God."

The second letter to the Corinthian church begins with, "Paul, an apostle of Jesus Christ by the will of God."

His message to the believers at Ephesus opens with practically the same words, testifying to his divine apostolic appointment and commission.

Writing to the Colossians, chapter 1, verse 1, he makes the same claim.

In I Timothy he opens with, "Paul, an apostle of Jesus Christ by the commandment of God."

II Timothy opens by declaring Paul's apostolic authority.

In writing to Titus he again asserts his claim to be an apostle ordained of God.

Galatians opens, "PAUL, AN APOSTLE (not of men, neither by man, but by Jesus Christ, and God the Father, who raised Him from the dead)."

Someone may be asking why all this personal reference; why this unusual emphasis. Why did Paul have to defend his authority as an apostle in every city where he preached? There are many reasons . . . we will name just a few:

Paul was not chosen by the apostolic band in Jerusalem--and you must not forget that they were human, just as we are. It was true then as it is true today, that in the religious realm men honor those whom they appoint. Today if a minister hopes to get very far in the denomination to which he belongs, he must seek the good graces of the religious leaders by allowing them to make his appointments and give to him his itinerary. Paul received his appointment directly from heaven, and therefore the apostles were just a little skeptical. They refused to take him into their arms wholeheartedly.

Again--Paul's message was not the apostolic message that the other apostles had been delivering. He preached a Gospel of the Grace of God, salvation provided for every creature, whereas the other apostles had ministered to the lost sheep of the house of Israel.

Paul's ministry was not exclusively for the Jews, and therefore the others were a bit hostile because of this. Paul preached to the Jews, to be sure--but he was a minister to the Gentiles, and his message was primarily for them.

There are other reasons which time and space will not permit us to discuss here--but these are the primary reasons why Paul met with opposition. He was bitterly opposed by the Judaizers and the legalizers, and the apostles at Jerusalem questioned his authority to be a minister of Jesus Christ. They refused to accept him as an apostle. They had already filled the vacancy left when Judas stepped out of the picture and committed suicide . . . they had cast lots and appointed Matthias to take the place of Judas. Please read Acts 1:15-26. Of course, when this was done, they did not have orders from Jesus Christ to hold such a meeting nor to have such an election; on the contrary, they violated the instructions Jesus had given to them . . . "And being assembled together with them, (Jesus) commanded them that they should not depart from Jerusalem, BUT WAIT FOR THE PROMISE OF THE FATHER, WHICH, SAITH HE, YE HAVE HEARD OF ME" (Acts 1:4). The apostles had strict instructions from Jesus to tarry, to wait for the Holy Ghost, before they moved one inch in the ministry left to them. They were commanded to do nothing until the coming of the Spirit, the Holy Ghost, who would lead them into all truth. There remained ten days from that time until Pentecost; but in spite of the command, "Do nothing until the Spirit comes to guide and direct you," the disciples did not wait for the Spirit. They immediately called a meeting, and in the energy of the flesh they elected a twelfth apostle. They were informed: "But ye shall receive power AFTER that the Holy Ghost is come upon you: and ye shall be witnesses . . ." (Acts 1:8). But they went ahead with their election.

Peter was the impatient one. I am sure that to him ten days seemed a long, long time to be without a twelfth apostle. He suggested that they elect someone to replace Judas. Instead of waiting as they had been instructed, they proceeded with the business of the Lord without the blessing of the Holy Ghost. Please read carefully Acts 1:15—26. You will find these words:

"And in those days (before the Holy Spirit came . . . before Pentecost) Peter stood up . . . and said . . . Men and brethren . . . of these men which have companied with us all the time that the Lord Jesus went in and out among us . . . must one be ordained to be a witness with us of HIS RESURRECTION" (Acts 1:15, 16, 21, 22).

In reading I Corinthians, especially chapter 15, you will note that God gave to Paul a very clear picture concerning the resurrection of Jesus Christ. It was Paul who said, "If there be no resurrection, our faith is vain, our preaching is vain, we are false witnesses, our loved ones who have died are perished, and there is no hope." This message was given to Paul to be preached to the church. Certainly the Head of the church is the Lord Jesus . . . crucified, buried, and risen. It is absolutely impossible for any person to be saved if he refuses to believe in the bodily resurrection of the Lord Jesus Christ. It was Paul who said, "That if thou shalt confess with thy mouth the Lord Jesus, and shalt believe in thine heart that God hath raised Him from the dead, thou shalt be saved" (Rom. 10:9).

Where did Peter get his authority to hold a meeting and elect a twelfth apostle? Where did he get his authority to *ordain* an apostle? Face it, beloved: Peter (like many of us, even ministers) did what he did in the energy of the flesh. Peter was not willing to wait for the Spirit to lead; he went ahead of the Spirit:

"And they appointed two, Joseph called Barsabas, who was surnamed Justus, and Matthias" (Acts 1:23).

Can you imagine the Holy Ghost setting up two men to be voted upon? If God Almighty calls a man, He appoints *a man*—not *two men* to be voted upon by other men. It is true that they prayed for the Lord to show them which one was to be chosen—but their prayer was wasted and empty, because they asked God to pick one of the candidates they had chosen. It seems they would have prayed for God to show them which one of the one hundred and twenty should be appointed to fill the place left by Judas. Why did they select only two, when there were one hundred and twenty of them waiting in the upper room for the coming of the Holy Spirit. They prayed, "Show which of these two . . . ." They did not get an answer; therefore they were forced to cast lots——or to vote——for the one to fill the place left vacant by the death of Judas. "And they gave forth their lots; and the lot fell upon Matthias; and he was numbered with the eleven apostles" (Acts 1:26).

Can you imagine these dear men voting, instead of waiting upon the Holy Spirit to appoint the apostle? The men who were there had been individually called by the Lord Jesus Christ, yet they were not willing to wait for Him to call one to take the place of Judas. I would like to point out here that a little later, the church was called upon to appoint the first foreign missionaries. Notice the record:

"Now there were in the church that was at Antioch certain prophets and teachers; as Barnabas, and Simeon that was called Niger, and Lucius of Cyrene, and Manaen, which had been brought up with Herod the tetrarch, and Saul. As they ministered to the Lord, and fasted, THE HOLY GHOST SAID, SEPARATE ME BARNABAS AND SAUL FOR THE WORK WHEREUNTO I HAVE CALLED THEM. And when they had fasted and prayed, and laid their hands on them, they sent them away. So they, being sent forth BY THE HOLY GHOST, departed unto Seleucia; and from thence they sailed to Cyprus" (Acts 13:1–4).

Please notice: At the close of a period of fasting and prayer, the church was instructed BY THE HOLY GHOST to appoint Barnabas and Saul as missionaries. You must agree that this was carried out in quite a different manner than casting lots to see who would go. Keep this in mind, beloved: In this age of grace (the dispensation of the Holy Ghost), it has pleased God, through the Holy Ghost, to call and ordain ministers, preachers, evangelists and leaders in the New Testament church. When a church "politics" for a pastor, mark it down: The blessings of God will not be upon that church! The Lord God Almighty is very capable of appointing ministers to preach the Gospel in the local assemblies where the Holy Spirit has right-of-way; and instead of "politicking" for ministers by ballot, they should be chosen after prayer and fasting. If any church will fast, pray, and seek God's will concerning a pastor, God will certainly help them choose the right man.

It is very clear that God did not recognize the choice of Matthias, because this dear man is never mentioned again in all the rest of the Bible. God ignored man's ordination—and after Pentecost, when the Holy Ghost had come, God chose HIS man to fill the place vacated by the betrayer, Judas Iscariot. God named Paul to be an apostle. It was not man's choice, but it was an outright call, commission, and ordination by Christ. Paul was ordained of God for the office of apostleship.

In I Timothy 2:7 Paul says he was *"ordained a preacher, and an apostle . . . a teacher of the Gentiles in faith and verity."* That is the paramount reason for the statement in Galatians 1:1: "NOT OF MEN, NEITHER BY MAN, BUT BY JESUS CHRIST, AND GOD THE FATHER, WHO RAISED HIM FROM THE DEAD."

If Paul should come to this land of ours today, he would be rejected by the ecclesiastical bosses. He would be rejected by the ecumenical movement. He would be declared "not cooperative." He would be classified as a "free lancer." It would be said of him, "He is not an apostle. We did not ordain him . . . he did not get his training at our seminaries. He is counterfeit. He was not officially chosen by us; we did not license him to preach in our denomination. We did not question him according to our doctrine, he does not have a degree from our seminary." That is exactly what they would say if the Apostle Paul came to town, organized a church and declared himself a minister of the Gospel.

Almost all of the first two chapters of Galatians is given over to the defense of (1) Paul's ministry, (2) Paul's method, and (3) his message of salvation by grace, through faith, plus nothing.

Galatians is the only one of the epistles written by Paul which is directed to a *group* of churches——that is, several local assemblies. All of his other epistles were directed to individuals . . . such as Timothy, Titus, Philemon . . . or to individual churches, one specific assembly such as the church at Rome, or to the believers at Corinth, Ephesus, Colosse, Philippi and Thessalonica. The epistle to the Galatians was passed from church to church, and several churches in Galatia and Asia Minor received this message from the Apostle to the Gentiles.

When Paul made his first missionary journey, he preached in the cities of Antioch, Iconium, Derbe and Lystra, and had wonderful success in leading men into a knowledge of the marvelous saving grace of God. These believers had gathered into local assemblies, had ordained elders, and were enjoying the liberty of salvation by grace through faith . . . saved by grace and kept by the power of God. That is, they enjoyed this liberty until the false teachers came and suggested to them that Paul was not an official apostle sent out by the church in Jerusalem. These legalizers began to preach that the Galatians must be circumcised after the Law of Moses, that they must keep the Law of Moses in order to be saved and stay saved. It was because of this that Paul wrote the letter to the Galatian churches.

In this letter, he answers the false doctrine of the legalizers, and declares that salvation is totally and entirely apart from the Law of Moses, apart from works, or from any effort on man's part. The new message delivered by Paul (received from God out of heaven but rejected by the legalizers and Judaizers in Jerusalem) was simply this: All men——Jews and Gentiles——are saved by grace. All men——Jews and Gentiles——are kept by grace. All men——Jews and Gentiles——are saved and kept, wholly and entirely apart from the works of the Law. The key word in the message delivered by Paul is "GRACE." The key verse in the epistle to the Galatians is Galatians 2:21: "I DO NOT FRUSTRATE THE GRACE OF GOD: FOR IF RIGHTEOUSNESS COME BY THE LAW, THEN CHRIST IS DEAD IN VAIN!"

According to the message delivered by the Apostle Paul, salvation is by faith in the person of the Lord Jesus Christ and in His finished work. Salvation is simply believing what the Bible tells us about Jesus——His birth, His life, His death, burial, and resurrection. Salvation is not "religion," it is not good works, it is not reformation. Salvation is not education. It is not culture nor is it a group of ordinances. Salvation is not a ritual or a ceremony. It is not prayers nor deeds of charity or good works. Salvation is the poor, bankrupt, hell-deserving, helpless, ungodly sinner, simply coming to Jesus in faith, believing that Jesus died for our sins "ACCORDING TO THE SCRIPTURES."

You and I will never be able to boast about our salvation. Why? Simply because "SALVATION IS OF THE LORD." Salvation is of the Lord, ALL of the Lord, ENTIRELY of the Lord. Jesus IS salvation: "Christ in you, the hope of glory!" (Col. 1:27).

We ministers today face the same problem Paul faced in Galatia. We still have with us preachers and churches who teach "salvation by grace——plus works," "by grace

—plus Law," "by grace—plus ordinances," "by grace—plus do's and dont's." But as for me in my ministry, I will stand by what the Bible says . . . "BUT TO HIM THAT WORKETH NOT, BUT BELIEVETH ON HIM THAT JUSTIFIETH THE UNGODLY, HIS FAITH IS COUNTED FOR RIGHTEOUSNESS" (Rom. 4:5).

Paul demonstrates his authority in Galatians 1:13 through Galatians 2:5.

Verses 13 and 14: "For ye have heard of my conversation in time past in the Jews' religion, how that beyond measure I persecuted the church of God, and wasted it: And profited in the Jews' religion above many my equals in mine own nation, being more exceedingly zealous of the traditions of my fathers."

The Greek word translated "conversation" here should have been translated "conduct" or "manner of life." The phrase used by Paul, "the Jews' religion" occurs twice here, and is referring to Judaism. The new dispensation (the Dispensation of Grace), having come, made the Mosaic system (or the practices of the Law of Moses) a mere "Jews' religion." Since the Lamb of God had been slain, there remained no more sacrifice for sin. Jesus offered Himself once, for all, forever, and of course the Jewish sacrifices and rituals became mere religious activity—or, as Paul states, "the Jews' religion."

Please notice Paul states that he was "far above" some people of his own nation in religious ability and activity. I suppose there was no better educated man than Paul in his day, and certainly there was no more zealous man. When he consented to the death of Stephen, and permitted the young men to lay their coats at his feet while they stoned Stephen, Saul thought he was doing God a favor. He thought the Christian religion was an enemy to the religion of his fathers; therefore he was exceedingly zealous in defending the religion of the Jews.

Verses 15 and 16: "But when it pleased God, who separated me from my mother's womb, and called me by His grace, to reveal His Son in me, that I might preach Him among the heathen; immediately I conferred not with flesh and blood."

The word "heathen" as used here means "Gentiles." Paul was slow to learn that from his birth God had chosen and dedicated him to preach the Gospel of the marvelous grace of God to the Gentiles.

Paul was a vessel chosen of God . . . even from his mother's womb. God called Paul, by His grace, to reveal His only begotten Son, and to preach to the Gentiles the Gospel of the death, burial and resurrection of Jesus.

I like what Paul says in verse 16: When he realized that God had called him as an apostle to the Gentiles, he said, "IMMEDIATELY I CONFERRED NOT WITH FLESH AND BLOOD: NEITHER WENT I UP TO JERUSALEM TO THEM WHICH WERE APOSTLES BEFORE ME; BUT I WENT INTO ARABIA, AND RETURNED AGAIN UNTO DAMASCUS." Paul did not seek the good graces of the ecclesiastical bosses, or the ecclesiastical group of his day. He did not ask them what to preach, where or when to preach. It is true that Paul spent the time between his conversion and the beginning of his public ministry, in Arabia; but he also spent a little time in Damascus. (Arabia reached almost up to the border of Damascus, but it did not include that city.)

You will recall it was in Damascus that Paul (who was at that time Saul of Tarsus) had been led by Ananias into the light of the glorious Gospel of salvation. God spoke to Ananias and made it clear that he was to tell

Saul of Tarsus the way of life. Immediately after his conversion, Paul began preaching in the synagogues in Damascus, affirming that Jesus was the Son of God. He continued to preach there until his life was threatened, and some of his friends, by night time, let him down in a basket over the wall to safety. Read the entire ninth chapter of Acts——especially verse 25.

Verse 18: "Then after three years I went up to Jerusalem to see Peter, and abode with him fifteen days."

The three years referred to in this verse are difficult to locate exactly; however, that is not important. Some believe it is the same time spoken of as "many days" in Acts 9:23. What Paul is trying to impress upon us is the fact that he preached the Gospel before he saw any of the apostles at Jerusalem; and that even when he did see them, he did not receive authority from them nor did they ordain him. His authority and ordination had already come from the Lord Jesus Christ. Paul wants it clearly understood that no man gave him his message or apostleship. . . . He was a chosen vessel, set apart to preach the good news of salvation by grace through faith plus nothing.

Verse 19: "But other of the apostles saw I none, save James the Lord's brother."

This was a very, very short visit. The apostolic band was not even called together. Paul saw only two disciples . . . Peter and James. Paul wants it clearly understood that he sought neither advice nor instruction from the disciple band.

Verse 20: "Now the things which I write unto you, behold, before God, I lie not."

Paul realizes the grave responsibility that rests upon him, and realizes that he is discussing eternal things

... very solemn things ... concerning the eternal destiny of men. He wants it clearly understood that he is speaking earnestly and truthfully as the Holy Ghost dictates to him. He wants it clearly understood that he is not a religionist--but a minister chosen and ordained of God. Paul was very careful always, that he tell the truth, the whole truth, defending the truth once delivered unto all faithful ministers.

In Romans 9:1 he begins by saying, "I say the truth in Christ, I lie not, my conscience also bearing me witness in the Holy Ghost." He wanted those to whom he preached to know that his message was truth--fresh from the altar of God Almighty, not sent out by a group of religious leaders or ecclesiastical bosses.

Verses 21-24: "Afterwards I came into the regions of Syria and Cilicia; and was unknown by face unto the churches of Judaea which were in Christ: but they had heard only, That he which persecuted us in times past now preacheth the faith which once he destroyed. AND THEY GLORIFIED GOD IN ME."

Thus we come to the end of chapter one. It would certainly be very interesting to know more about this Syrian and Cilician ministry; but for some reason the Holy Spirit did not see fit to enlighten us more at this particular point. Paul is hurriedly reviewing his ministry as an apostle. He is doing this to demonstrate the fact that authority in the spiritual realm is derived and received from Almighty God, and not from men. It is refreshing to note that in all that Paul did, he sought no glory or praise from men for himself, but he was always glad to record the fact that men glorified God in him ... that is, they glorified God when they heard the message God had given to Paul for them.

Note verse 23: The people of Syria and Cilicia had

not seen the face of Paul, but had heard that "the man who persecuted us in times past now preacheth the faith which once he destroyed!"

GALATIANS -- CHAPTER TWO

1. Then fourteen years after I went up again to Jerusalem with Barnabas, and took Titus with me also.

2. And I went up by revelation, and communicated unto them that gospel which I preach among the Gentiles, but privately to them which were of reputation, lest by any means I should run, or had run, in vain.

3. But neither Titus, who was with me, being a Greek, was compelled to be circumcised:

4. And that because of false brethren unawares brought in, who came in privily to spy out our liberty which we have in Christ Jesus, that they might bring us into bondage:

5. To whom we gave place by subjection, no, not for an hour; that the truth of the gospel might continue with you.

6. But of these who seemed to be somewhat, (whatsoever they were, it maketh no matter to me: God accepteth no man's person:) for they who seemed to be somewhat in conference added nothing to me:

7. But contrariwise, when they saw that the gospel of the uncircumcision was committed unto me, as the gospel of the circumcision was unto Peter;

8. (For he that wrought effectually in Peter to the apostleship of the circumcision, the same was mighty in me toward the Gentiles:)

9. And when James, Cephas, and John, who seemed to be pillars, perceived the grace that was given unto me, they gave to me and Barnabas the right hands of fellowship; that we should go unto the heathen, and they unto the circumcision.

10. Only they would that we should remember the poor; the same which I also was forward to do.

11. But when Peter was come to Antioch, I withstood him to the face, because he was to be blamed.

12. For before that certain came from James, he did eat with the Gentiles: but when they were come, he withdrew and separated himself, fearing them which were of the circumcision.

13. And the other Jews dissembled likewise with him; insomuch that Barnabas also was carried away with their dissimulation.

14. But when I saw that they walked not uprightly according to the truth of the gospel, I said unto Peter before them all, If thou, being a Jew, livest after the manner of Gentiles, and not as do the Jews, why compellest thou the Gentiles to live as do the Jews?

15. We who are Jews by nature, and not sinners of the Gentiles,

16. Knowing that a man is not justified by the works of the law, but by the faith of Jesus Christ, even we have believed in Jesus Christ, that we might be justified by the faith of Christ, and not by the works of the law: for by the works of the law shall no flesh be justified.

17. But if, while we seek to be justified by Christ, we ourselves also are found sinners, is therefore Christ the minister of sin? God forbid.

18. For if I build again the things which I destroyed, I make myself a transgressor.

19. For I through the law am dead to the law, that I might live unto God.

20. I am crucified with Christ: nevertheless I live; yet not I, but Christ liveth in me: and the life which I now live in the flesh I live by the faith of the Son of God, who loved me, and gave himself for me.

21. I do not frustrate the grace of God: for if righteousness come by the law, then Christ is dead in vain.

Verse 1: "Then fourteen years after I went up again to Jerusalem with Barnabas, and took Titus with me also."

This brings us to the visit of Paul, Barnabas, and Titus to the city of Jerusalem . . . the visit so clearly described for us in chapter fifteen of the Acts of the Apostles. The issue of circumcision had been brought up by the legalizers (Judaizers and false teachers who probably claimed to represent the mother church in Jerusalem). They had declared that the disciples at Antioch and Syria were not really saved at all because they had not yet submitted to the Law of Moses and the rituals of Judaism. I trust you will read the entire fifteenth chapter of Acts. Read it carefully, thoroughly, and become familiar with the important matters discussed at the council in Jerusalem.

Verse 2: "And I went up by revelation, and communicated unto them that Gospel which I preach among the Gentiles, but privately to them which were of reputation, lest by any means I should run, or had run, in vain."

Please notice the first part of verse 2: "And I went up by revelation." Paul simply means that he went up according to the revealed will of God. That was the program of the Apostle Paul——and it is the program of every normal Christian. Whether we eat, or drink——or whatsoever we do, we should do it all to the glory of God. We should never do anything according to *our* will or *our* program. We should always seek the will of God and the guiding hand of the Holy Ghost. Paul declares that he communicated unto them "THAT GOSPEL WHICH I PREACH AMONG THE GENTILES." In other words, when he arrived at the great council meeting he did not minimize the fact that he had been preaching the new message of "salvation by grace through faith plus nothing." He cut no corners, he feared no consequences; he laid the truth down, line upon line, and told the ecclesiastical leaders exactly what he had been preaching to the Gentiles. Paul knew the situation was serious, and would be very difficult to solve . . . that only through the Holy Ghost could it BE solved. There was great danger that the progress of the Gospel could be hindered by this terrible conflict between salvation by grace through faith, and Judaism. Paul sought the cooperation of the apostles, rather than their opposition. He wanted their good graces, not their scorn––but he did not compromise the message of grace to *obtain* their good graces. He stood firm on the one foundation: Jesus Christ–– crucified, buried, and risen "according to the Scripture," and "Christ in you, the hope of glory."––The only hope for any poor sinner, regardless of race, creed, or color, is the grace of God––Christ in your heart by faith.

Verses 3–5: "But neither Titus, who was with me, being a Greek, was compelled to be circumcised: and that because of false brethren unawares brought in, who came in privily to spy out our liberty which we have in Christ Jesus, that they might bring us into bondage: to whom we gave place by subjection, no, not for an hour; that the truth of the Gospel might continue with you."

What Paul is saying here is simply this: "Not even Titus, who was with me, being a Greek, was compelled to be circumcised." At another time, under different circumstances and under other conditions, Paul had taken Timothy and circumcised him. He did it on the principle of being "all things to all men, that I might by all means save some" (Acts 16:3; I Cor. 9:22). Read both of these verses carefully.

But when the apostles in Jerusalem insisted that Titus must be circumcised as a condition of spiritual fellowship, Paul refused to surrender to their demands. He stood his ground, in order that the truth of the Gospel of "salvation by grace" through faith minus works might continue to be preached and practiced. Certainly we should thank God for Paul's actions in such a serious time as that was.

Paul was not a religious hot-head or fanatic. At another time, as I have already stated, he permitted Timothy to be circumcised. He loved his people so much (Rom. 9:1–3) that he was willing to do anything and everything possible to reach his own nation with the Gospel of grace; but when he realized the danger presented by such practices (the danger of frustrating the grace of God, or adding to the Gospel of grace) he flatly refused to permit Titus to be circumcised. He declared that false brethren had been brought in without his knowing it (". . . brought in privily to spy out our liberty" of grace). He said, "We gave place by subjection, no, not for one hour, that the truth of the Gospel might continue with you." He did not compromise with them one iota. He stood firm and refused to permit the circumcision of Titus, even though he (Titus) was a Greek.

Verses 6–10: "But of these who seemed to be somewhat, (whatsoever they were, it maketh no matter to me: God accepteth no man's person:) for they who seemed to be somewhat in conference added nothing to me: But contrariwise, when they saw that the Gospel of the uncircumcision was committed unto me, as the Gospel of the circumcision was unto Peter; (For He that wrought effectually in Peter to the apostleship of the circumcision, the same was mighty in me toward the Gentiles:) And when James, Cephas, and John, who seemed to be pillars, perceived the grace that was given unto me, they gave to me and Barnabas the right hands of fellowship; that we should go unto the heathen, and they unto the circumcision. Only they would that we should remember the poor; the same which I also was forward to do."

Beloved, it always pays to stand up for Jesus. It never pays to compromise. Paul's authority was recognized and acknowledged by the apostles at the council in Jerusalem. Be sure to read Acts chapter 15 . . . study it carefully, and you will note that Paul stood up for the Gospel of the grace of God. He declared that the Christian is not under the Law of Moses, that the Law of Moses does not help save the Christian, and that the Law of Moses does not help *keep* one saved. He stood up for the truth that the gospel of the Law neither saves us, nor helps to save us; neither keeps us nor helps to keep us. Paul declared to the council there that the Law of Moses was neither his means of life, nor was it his rule of life; but it was emphasized in the council at Jerusalem that the believer should be careful in the exercise of the liberty provided in the grace of God. The Christian should be very careful to avoid (if at all possible) anything that would cause a weak brother to stumble. Please read Romans 14:1 through Romans 15:3. Also read I Corinthians 8, verses 1 through 13.

After much debating at the council in Jerusalem, the conclusion was reached that God had called Peter to minister to the nation of Israel, but that God had called and commissioned Paul to minister to the Gentiles (Rom.

11:13). They decided that Paul should go to the heathen (the Gentiles) and that they (the apostles) would go unto the circumcision. Peter and the other apostles extended the right hand of fellowship to Paul, thereby acknowledging the authority of the Gospel of grace . . . that there was no difference between the Jew and the Gentile, but that in this dispensation of the grace of God, all must be saved alike: By grace, through faith in the finished work of Jesus, without the deeds of the Law, without the practices of Judaism.

Verse 11: "But when Peter was come to Antioch, I withstood him to the face, because he was to be blamed."

Peter had made a remarkable address at the council meeting in Jerusalem. He sanctioned Paul's position concerning grace . . . that the Christian believer is not under the Law of Moses. Read Acts 15:7—11. But when Peter came to visit Paul in Antioch, he changed his tune! He took a different attitude, for which Peter truly "WAS TO BE BLAMED."

After the meeting at Jerusalem, it had seemed that the matter was settled. Peter, quite happy over his newfound liberty in the grace of God, decided he would pay a visit to the believers at Antioch, and there would demonstrate his agreement with the Apostle Paul concerning the liberty of the grace of God. But when he went to Antioch, something happened which caused Paul to openly rebuke Peter. Paul exclaimed in the presence of Peter, concerning his own personal relationship to the Law of Moses, "FOR I THROUGH THE LAW AM DEAD TO THE LAW!" (Gal. 2:19). What a statement! What a tremendous testimony! Paul did not say, "The LAW is dead" . . . indeed, he did not. He said, "I am dead TO the Law!" Of course, Paul is speaking of God's holy Law, including the commandments written upon the tables of stone. So far as that Law is concerned, Paul said, "I am dead." That is, "In the eyes of the Law, I (Paul) do not exist any longer. The Law does not even recognize my existence." Paul did not say, "The Law is dead," no, no. It is definitely true that the Law is very much alive. The Law still curses, it still condemns, it still is the ministration of death. The Law demands the death penalty for sin; but Paul declared, "So far as I am concerned, the Law cannot touch me any more. I am beyond the reach of the Law of Moses forever! I through the Law am dead to the Law. What I could never have done in my flesh, Jesus did for me" (Rom. 8:1–4).

In Romans 7:4 Paul declares, "Wherefore, my brethren, ye also are become dead to the Law by the body of Christ." You see, what Paul enjoyed, *we also* enjoy in Christ . . . that is, if we are a true believer.

Again––in Romans 6:14: ". . . for ye are not under the Law, but under grace." Every born again believer is under grace . . . not under Law.

In Galatians 2:20, Paul puts it this way: "I am crucified with Christ: nevertheless I live; yet not I, but Christ liveth in me: and the life which I now live in the flesh I live by the faith of the Son of God, who loved me, and gave Himself for me." Yes, Paul said, "I am dead to the Law––but I am alive unto God." He spoke these words in response to certain inconsistent men–– especially the Apostle Peter at Antioch. Paul had been preaching "Grace, Grace, Grace . . . salvation by Grace, entirely apart from the Law . . . salvation by faith in the finished work of the Lord Jesus, plus nothing." He had taught that the Gentile believers were not under the Law of Moses, but that they were saved by grace *apart from* the Law of Moses, sanctified by grace and kept by grace, apart from the Law of Moses. Peter also, when he came up to visit the believers at Antioch, endorsed the message of Paul and entered into full Christian fellowship with the Gentile believers, on the basis that they were saved by grace alone. Then shortly, a group of legalistic, proselyting Law-preachers came up from the mother church in Jerusalem, in order to spy on Paul and his liberty in the grace of God. Peter, being afraid because of these legalistic preachers, immediately became so frightened that he withdrew himself from the Gentile believers and put himself back under the Law of Moses. Paul became so righteously indignant that he openly rebuked Peter, and as we would say today, Paul "laid him out."

Peter reminds me of some of the fellows today. His error was two-fold: When he was with Jews, he followed the conduct of the Jew; when he was with Gentiles, he took the place of a Gentile under grace. He was under Law one day and under grace the next. Certainly he was living a very inconsistent life, and Paul knew it. Paul severely rebuked him . . . and he did it publicly. Suppose we let Paul tell us about it:

Verses 12—14: "For before that certain came from James, he did eat with the Gentiles: but when they were come, he withdrew and separated himself, fearing them which were of the circumcision. And the other Jews dissembled likewise with him; insomuch that Barnabas also was carried away with their dissimulation. But when I saw that they walked not uprightly according to the truth of the Gospel, I said unto Peter before them all, If thou, being a Jew, livest after the manner of Gentiles, and not as do the Jews, why compellest thou the Gentiles to live as do the Jews?"

Certainly this action on the part of Peter is hard to understand, and hard to explain; but we must remember that after all, Peter was a man of like passions as we are. Even though the Roman Catholics claim Peter as their first Pope (they say he was the vicar of Christ and the head of the church . . . they claim their popes to be infallible), Peter certainly was not infallible on this occasion!

We need to notice verse 13 carefully: Other Jews likewise walked away——even Barnabas was carried away with their dissimulation. So the Apostle Paul was left alone. He often stood alone, declaring the liberty "wherewith Christ hath made us free" (Gal. 5:1). So it was here, as in instances before. He stood, and he refused to compromise. Thank God for the Apostle Paul . . . a man who feared no one except the Lord God who called and ordained him! Even though they all walked away, including his bosom friend and companion Barnabas, Paul stood firm.

In verse 14, we learn that Paul did not use the soft pedal in rebuking Peter. He said to Peter (before all of the Jews): "Peter, if you are a Jew, living after the manner of Gentiles and not as do the Jews, why do you compel the Gentiles to live as Jews live?" I think the words of Paul are easily understood, and I think we need not call up Dr. Sounding Brass or Theologian Tinkling Cymbal, to ask them to interpret these words for us. Paul said to Peter, "Why do you live one way, and command others to live another way?" The same is true today. Ministers bind burdens upon their parishioners that the ministers themselves cannot bear . . . rules and regulations are laid down that preachers could not keep if they tried——yet they command their parishioners to practice their rules and regulations. Paul rebuked Peter to his face, before all of the people.

To sum up the matter, we can clearly see and understand that the Galatians knew that Paul was certainly not seeking popularity. He was not seeking glory for himself. Paul puts his own character and ability in the background, and boldly declares that his Gospel of Grace was revealed directly from God . . . it did not come through man. As for the Judaizers, this man Paul had been an outstanding Judaist. He was a Jew, but he had forsaken Judaism for Christianity——which was, to him, something much better. Paul preached the grace of God for many years before he saw any one of the other apostles. When he DID meet the others, they had nothing to add to his Gospel of Grace, because the Gospel of the marvelous grace of God is the last word from Heaven, revealed to the Apostle Paul . . . the ordained minister to the Gentiles.

Finally, after the council in Jerusalem, the other disciples recognized Paul's divine apostleship. According to Galatians 2:11—14, Peter had nothing to say when he was severely rebuked by Paul. Certainly he had made a sad mistake in his actions at Antioch, but he did not speak up in defense of his authority for such action.

PAUL DECLARES JUSTIFICATION BY FAITH WITHOUT LAW—WORKS

Paul declares that both Jews and Gentiles are on the same grounds, insofar as sin and salvation are concerned.

Verses 15 and 16: "We who are Jews by nature, and not sinners of the Gentiles, knowing that a man is not justified by the works of the Law, but by the faith of Jesus Christ, even we have believed in Jesus Christ, that we might be justified by the faith of Christ, and not by the works of the Law: for by the works of the Law shall no flesh be justified."

Paul points out here that it is not a question of justification for the Gentiles any more than it is a question of justification for the Jew also, because Jews and Gentiles in this dispensation of grace are justified before God in the same way . . . by grace, through faith, plus nothing. It will be a happy day in the lives of some church people when they realize the difference between justification "BEFORE GOD" (Rom. 4:2), which is by faith alone, which saves the sinner, causing him to become a Christian; and justification "BEFORE MEN" (James 2:14–26), which is by works and which gives the believer a testimony before his fellowman. Through good works he proves to his fellowman that living faith abides in his heart. We are justified *before God* by naked faith; we are justified *before men* through good faithful works . . . stewardship. Jesus commanded, "Let your light so shine before men that they may see your good works and glorify your Father which is in heaven." Works do not have anything to do with justification before God. We are justified by faith without the deeds of the Law: "Therefore we conclude that a man is justified by faith without the deeds of the law" (Rom. 3:28). "Not of works, lest any man should boast" (Eph. 2:9). "Not by works of righteousness which we have done, but according to His mercy He saved us, by the washing of regeneration, and renewing of the Holy Ghost" (Titus 3:5).

Jew or Gentile, by the deeds of the Law there shall no flesh be justified. Paul clearly states this again in Romans 3:20. Here he is saying to the Jews that if they hope to stand before God in peace, they too must come by grace through faith, and not by the works of the Law —or by the practice of Judaism.

Verse 17: "But if, while we seek to be justified by Christ, we ourselves also are found sinners, is therefore Christ the minister of sin? God forbid!"

You will notice in Paul's writings that he many times asks a question, and then answers his own question immediately. In Paul's day it was customary for the Jews to speak of Gentiles as "sinners." Of course, many times they were referred to as "dogs." Paul knew that some Jew——perhaps even Peter——was asking, "If we Jews turn from our religion and seek to be justified before God by faith in Jesus Christ alone, if we turn our backs upon the works of the Law, then will we not put ourselves in the same class with Gentile sinners? And if we do that, does that not make Christ the minister of sin? Would it not then be Christ who makes us sinners?" Paul answers, "God forbid!"

Verse 18: "For if I build again the things which I destroyed, I make myself a transgressor."

Paul's reply to such a question as that of the preceding verse, is this: "It is not Christ who makes us sinners——it is we ourselves . . . because if, after seeking justification through the finished work of Jesus Christ, we again turn to the Law of Moses as if we were still *unjustified* sinners seeking to become justified by the works of the Law, we are then transgressors of the Law and therefore we make ourselves sinners . . . because sin is the transgression of God's Law." Read I John 3:4.

Never entertain the idea that Paul was against the Law of God. He testifies in Romans that the Law of God is holy and righteous. Jesus came, not to destroy the Law, but to fulfill the Law——and what Paul was preaching is simply this: "In Jesus we are Law-keepers. In Jesus we satisfy the Law of God——but ONLY IN JESUS; because what the Law could not do, what the Law had never done, Jesus did in a body like unto your body and mine." No, Paul was not minimizing the holiness and the power of the Law. He was simply attempting to set straight the people who had been confused by the legalizers who had been commanding believers to practice Law-works to complete their salvation and to be able to keep their salvation. Paul was one hundred percent against mixing Law and Grace. Paul preached pure Grace, and ONLY pure Grace, for salvation.

Verse 19: "For I through the Law am dead to the Law, that I might live unto God."

Is the believer under Law? Is the Christian subject to the Law of Moses? In Paul's day, that question was already a burning issue. The Bible is crystal clear in giving the answer to the question, "Is the believer under the Law?" Paul answers: "We are not under Law, but under Grace" (Rom. 6:14). The believer is loosed and delivered from the Law (Rom. 7:2). The believer is delivered from the Law (Rom. 7:6). The Lord Jesus Christ is the end of the Law for righteousness to everyone that believeth (Rom. 10:4). The Christian is free from the Law (Rom. 8:2). And in our present Scripture (Gal. 2:19) the believer is "DEAD TO THE LAW."

It may be that some of the Jews asked Paul, "When and where did you die?" The answer is found in our next verse:

Verse 20: "I am crucified with Christ: nevertheless I live; yet not I, but Christ liveth in me: and the life which I now live in the flesh I live by the faith of the Son of God, who loved me, and gave Himself for me."

Paul answers by saying, "I died when Jesus died on the cross." When Jesus hung on the cross, the passers-by saw only *one* man dying on a cross; but God the Father saw *more* than one man. God saw more than a physical body. God saw the spiritual body, the mystical body——and that body is Christ. The church of the living

God is the body of Christ. God looks upon the church as a body. Jesus is the Head; we born again believers are the members. In I Corinthians 12:13, Paul declares, "For by one Spirit are we all baptized into one body, *whether we be Jews or Gentiles.*"

Writing to the believers at Ephesus, Paul said, "For we are members of His body, OF HIS FLESH AND OF HIS BONES."

Writing to the believers in Colosse, Paul said, "And He is the head of the body, the church, who is the beginning, the firstborn from the dead; that in all things He might have the preeminence."

Christ is the head of the church; we are members of His body. Colossians 3:3: "Ye are dead, and your life is hid with Christ in God." As God looked down upon Mount Calvary and saw the Lord Jesus dying on the cross, He saw not only the head of the body, but God saw the entire body——complete, without spot or wrinkle or any such thing (Eph. 5:27). He saw the glorious church that He purchased with His own blood. God lives in the eternal present. He knows the end in the beginning; and He saw in Christ the church . . . complete, without spot, the holy church that will be displayed in the heavenlies throughout eternity (Eph. 2:7).

"Blessed be the God and Father of our Lord Jesus Christ, who hath blessed us with all spiritual blessings in heavenly places in Christ: according as He hath chosen us in Him before the foundation of the world, that we should be holy and without blame before Him in love: having predestinated us unto the adoption of children by Jesus Christ to Himself, according to the good pleasure of His will" (Eph. 1:3–5).

That is the meaning of the words of Paul, "For I

through the Law am dead to the Law." He died when Jesus died on the cross. Paul, by grace, was in Christ as He hung on the cross, and what happened to Jesus on the cross happened to Paul since he was in Christ. What happened to Paul happened to every born again believer from then until this day, and to every believer from this day until the church is completed and caught up to meet Jesus in the air.

"WHEREFORE, my brethren, ye also are become dead to the Law BY THE BODY OF CHRIST" (Rom. 7:4).

The Law could do no more——it had no more authority over Paul. Certainly the Law holds nothing against a dead man——("I am dead to the Law . . . I am crucified with Christ"). If a person commits murder, the state tries him as a criminal, the judge sentences him to die in the gas chamber, and the sentence is carried out. When the corpse of the murderer is removed from the gas chamber . . . when the body is buried . . . the courts hold nothing against the dead man. He paid the supreme penalty of death. Jesus Christ, the Son of God, paid the penalty for sin ("The wages of sin is death"). Jesus died for sinners. He knew no sin (II Cor. 5:21). He was the sinless, spotless, Son of God. He willingly died on the cross, that we might be saved, and all believers died with Him because in reality all believers were in Him when He laid down His life on the cross. But that is not all:

When Jesus was pronounced dead, Joseph of Arimathea went with Nicodemus to Pilate and asked for His body, in order that they might bury Him. The record is found in Matthew 27:58—60:

"He went to Pilate, and begged the body of Jesus. Then Pilate commanded the body to be delivered. And when Joseph had taken the body, he wrapped it in a clean linen cloth, and laid it in his own new tomb, which he had hewn out in the rocks."

Beloved, notice the word "BODY." Please notice that word is used three times in the account we have just read. The "body" of Jesus was begged for burial, Pilate surrendered the "body," they wrapped the "body" in clean cloth, they buried it in Joseph's new tomb. We born again believers are crucified, buried, and risen with Jesus. What He experienced, we experienced with Him:

"Know ye not, that so many of us as were baptized into Jesus Christ were baptized into His death? Therefore we are buried with Him by baptism into death: that like as Christ was raised up from the dead by the glory of the Father, even so we also should walk in newness of life" (Rom. 6:3–4). Yes, born again believers are crucified with Christ, buried with Christ in the baptism of His death. (Certainly Paul is not referring to the water in the River Jordan nor to the water in a baptistry. The baptism referred to in this scripture is the baptism of which Jesus spoke when He said, "I have a baptism to be baptized with.")

When Jesus came out of that tomb, every member of the New Testament church came out with Him . . . that is, we were raised from the dead along with the Head of the church:

"Now if we be dead with Christ, we believe that we shall also live with Him: knowing that Christ being raised from the dead dieth no more; death hath no more dominion over Him. For in that He died, He died unto sin once: but in that He liveth, He liveth unto God. Likewise reckon ye also yourselves to be dead indeed unto sin, but alive unto God through Jesus Christ our Lord" (Rom. 6:8–11).

Hear these precious words: "If ye then be risen

with Christ, seek those things which are above, where Christ sitteth on the right hand of God. Set your affection on things above, not on things on the earth. FOR YE ARE DEAD, AND YOUR LIFE IS HID WITH CHRIST IN GOD" (Col. 3:1–3).

But that is not all. Hear this:

"But God, who is rich in mercy, for His great love wherewith He loved us, even when we were dead in sins, hath quickened us together with Christ, (by grace ye are saved;) AND HATH RAISED US UP TOGETHER, AND MADE US SIT TOGETHER IN HEAVENLY PLACES IN CHRIST JESUS" (Eph. 2:4–6).

Positionally, we born again believers sit with Jesus in heavenly places—*now*. Our Head is in heaven, the Body to which we belong is in heaven, the Foundation of the New Testament church is in heaven. Our citizenship is in heaven. We sit together in heavenly places in Christ Jesus. What a wonderful position! It is tragic that so many professing Christians do not understand the marvel and the miracle of the grace of God. They have been misled by modern legalizers who put them under commandments. They worry, they struggle, they work, they toil, they strive, they endure . . . in an effort to keep saved! They are trying desperately to "make it in." True believers are *already* "in" . . . we are SEATED WITH JESUS IN HEAVENLY PLACES. We are members of His body, bone of His bone, flesh of His flesh.

"For what the Law could not do, in that it was weak through the flesh, God sending His own Son in the likeness of sinful flesh, and for sin, condemned sin in the flesh: that the righteousness of the Law might be fulfilled in us . . ." (Rom. 8:3–4).

"FOR CHRIST IS THE END OF THE LAW FOR

RIGHTEOUSNESS TO EVERY ONE THAT BELIEVETH" (Rom. 10:4).

Those who are authorities concerning the Greek language tell us that Galatians 2:20 should read: "I have been crucified with Christ . . . and it is no longer I that live, but Christ liveth in me: and that life which I now live in the flesh, I live in faith, the faith which is in the Son of God, who loved me and gave Himself for me."

The Law of Moses demanded death as the righteous penalty for all sin. The Law executed its sentence and claimed its demand upon Paul in the person of the Lord Jesus Christ, the Lamb of God, the substitute for sinners . . . He who died on the cross on Golgotha's hill. God reckoned Paul in Christ——and put Paul to death in Christ when Christ died on the cross for Paul. Jesus represented Paul on the cross. Jesus also represented YOU, if you are a believer——and He *wants* to represent every sinner who may read these lines. If you are lost, Jesus is seeking you through this message. If you will believe on Jesus He will justify you before God, because Jesus is the "propitiation for our sins, and not for ours only, but also for the sins of the whole world" (I John 2:2).

Paul declares, "We thus judge (reckon) that if One died for all, then were all dead: and that He died for all, that they which live should not henceforth live unto themselves, but unto Him which died for them, and rose again" (II Cor. 5:14—15).

Therefore, according to God's reckoning at Calvary, we died in the Lord Jesus; but we did not remain dead. We arose from the dead when God raised up Christ from the dead, and we (believers) who died in Christ were also brought to life in Christ, because He is life: "I am the Way, the Truth, and the Life" (John 14:6). We believers were quickened together with Christ (Eph. 2:5).

Therefore, we were crucified with Christ, we were raised with Christ, we now live in Christ because He is our life.

Since "Faith cometh by hearing and hearing by the Word of God," *and*

"In the beginning was the Word, and the Word was with God, and the Word was God," *and*

"The Word became flesh and dwelt among us," *and*

Since that Word was Jesus, the only begotten Son of God, *and*

Since He died on the cross, *and*

If we believe in Him we become a member of His body, bone of His bone and flesh of His flesh, we can say that we live "In faith, THE faith, which is IN the Son of God."

What I have said is simply this: It is *Christ in you*, the hope of glory (Col. 1:27). It is you in Christ, the hope of heaven (Col. 3:3). "There is therefore now no condemnation to them which are in Christ Jesus"; so, the only position that makes you eligible to stand before a holy God is that of being in Christ by faith. When we accept His finished work, we receive everything purchased through His finished work; because it is Christ in you—and Christ is a person. You do not receive Jesus "in parts" or on the "installment plan." He is a personality, and when you receive Jesus, you receive all of Him. When you are born again you are *completely* born again. We are not saved in parts, a little at a time; we are saved when Jesus enters the heart by faith.

When Paul died in Christ, Paul met all the righteous requirements and *commands* of the Law. From that moment forward, he was forever delivered from the *penalty* of the Law. The Law had put Paul to death——but it was not the Law that brought him back to life. The Law was neither the means of his life, nor was the Law the rule of his life. The Law was "done away" in Christ Jesus (II Cor. 3:11). That is the reason Paul said, "The life I now live in the flesh, I live by the faith of the Son of God who loved me, and gave Himself for me!"

Verse 21: "I do not frustrate the grace of God: for if righteousness come by the Law, then Christ is dead in vain."

What Paul is saying in this verse is simply this: "If a man could have been saved by obeying the Law . . . if a man could attain righteousness on his own merits through keeping the Law, then certainly there was no need for Jesus to die on the cross!" Jesus died because of man's utter inability to save himself. The death of Jesus was an imperative on behalf of man. The natural man cannot know God, cannot understand God, and cannot receive God. No man can come to God except the Spirit draw him (John 6:44) and the instrument through which the Spirit convicts, convinces, and draws, is the Word of God. The Word of God is Christ, because it was the Word that became flesh and tabernacled among us. The natural man cannot please God (Rom. 8:8–9); therefore it was imperative that Jesus take a body, and in that body do for man what man could never have done for himself.

You precious people who mix Law and Grace, who thunder out long and loud that we must keep the Law and live by the commandments, hear these solemn words:

"Forasmuch as ye are manifestly declared to be the epistle of Christ ministered by us, written not with ink, but with the Spirit of the living God; not in tables of stone, but in fleshy tables of the heart. And such trust have we through Christ to God-ward: not that we are sufficient of ourselves to think any thing as of ourselves; but our sufficiency is of God; who also hath made us able ministers of the new testament; not of the letter, but of the spirit: FOR THE LETTER KILLETH, BUT THE SPIRIT GIVETH LIFE. But if the ministration of death, written and engraven in stones, was glorious, so that the children of Israel could not stedfastly behold the face of Moses for the glory of his countenance; WHICH GLORY WAS TO BE DONE AWAY: How shall not the ministration of the spirit be rather glorious? For if the ministration of condemnation be glory, much more doth the ministration of righteousness exceed in glory. For even that which was made glorious had no glory in this respect, by reason of the glory that excelleth. For if that which is done away was glorious, much more that which remaineth is glorious. Seeing then that we have such hope, we use great plainness of speech. And not as Moses, which put a vail over his face, that the children of Israel could not stedfastly look to the end of that which is abolished: But their minds were blinded: for until this day remaineth the same vail untaken away in the reading of the old testament; which vail is done away in Christ." (Beloved, can you not see the clear truth set forth here?) "But even unto this day, when Moses is read, the vail is upon their heart. Nevertheless when it shall turn to the Lord, the vail shall be taken away. Now the Lord is that Spirit: and where the Spirit of the Lord is, THERE IS LIBERTY. But we all, with open face beholding as in a glass the glory of the Lord, are changed into the same image from glory to glory, EVEN AS BY THE SPIRIT OF THE LORD" (II Cor. 3:3–18).

Here Paul is saying to us that the believer is not transformed into the image of Christ by the works (or practices) of the Law; but by the Holy Ghost abiding in his bosom. It is the Spirit that giveth life, not the letter of the Law; because the letter of the Law killeth . . . it is the ministration of death . . . the ministration of condemnation. But the Spirit quickeneth us together with Christ . . . and every born again believer possesses the Holy Ghost! (Rom. 8:9).

"Let no man therefore judge you in meat, or in drink, or in respect of an holyday, or of the new moon, or of the sabbath days: which are a shadow of things to come; but the body is of Christ" (Col. 3:16—17).

GALATIANS — CHAPTER THREE

1. O foolish Galatians, who hath bewitched you, that ye should not obey the truth, before whose eyes Jesus Christ hath been evidently set forth, crucified among you?

2. This only would I learn of you, Received ye the Spirit by the works of the law, or by the hearing of faith?

3. Are ye so foolish? having begun in the Spirit, are ye now made perfect by the flesh?

4. Have ye suffered so many things in vain? if it be yet in vain.

5. He therefore that ministereth to you the Spirit, and worketh miracles among you, doeth he it by the works of the law, or by the hearing of faith?

6. Even as Abraham believed God, and it was accounted to him for righteousness.

7. Know ye therefore that they which are of faith, the same are the children of Abraham.

8. And the scripture, foreseeing that God would justify the heathen through faith, preached before the gospel unto Abraham, saying, In thee shall all nations be blessed.

9. So then they which be of faith are blessed with faithful Abraham.

10. For as many as are of the works of the law are under the curse: for it is written, Cursed is every one that continueth not in all things which are written in the book of the law to do them.

11. But that no man is justified by the law in the sight of God, it is evident: for, The just shall live by faith.

12. And the law is not of faith: but, The man that doeth them shall live in them.

13. Christ hath redeemed us from the curse of the law, being made a curse for us: for it is written, Cursed is every one that hangeth on a tree:

14. That the blessing of Abraham might come on the Gentiles through Jesus Christ; that we might receive the promise of the Spirit through faith.

15. Brethren, I speak after the manner of men; Though it be but a man's covenant, yet if it be confirmed, no man disannulleth, or addeth thereto.

16. Now to Abraham and his seed were the promises made. He saith not, And to seeds, as of many; but as of one, And to thy seed, which is Christ.

17. And this I say, that the covenant, that was confirmed before of God in Christ, the law, which was four hundred and thirty years after, cannot disannul, that it should make the promise of none effect.

18. For if the inheritance be of the law, it is no more of promise: but God gave it to Abraham by promise.

19. Wherefore then serveth the law? It was added because of transgressions, till the seed should come to whom the promise was made;

and it was ordained by angels in the hand of a mediator.

20. Now a mediator is not a mediator of one, but God is one.

21. Is the law then against the promises of God? God forbid: for if there had been a law given which could have given life, verily righteousness should have been by the law.

22. But the scripture hath concluded all under sin, that the promise by faith of Jesus Christ might be given to them that believe.

23. But before faith came, we were kept under the law, shut up unto the faith which should afterwards be revealed.

24. Wherefore the law was our schoolmaster to bring us unto Christ, that we might be justified by faith.

25. But after that faith is come, we are no longer under a schoolmaster.

26. For ye are all the children of God by faith in Christ Jesus.

27. For as many of you as have been baptized into Christ have put on Christ.

28. There is neither Jew nor Greek, there is neither bond nor free, there is neither male nor female: for ye are all one in Christ Jesus.

29. And if ye be Christ's, then are ye Abraham's seed, and heirs according to the promise.

THE GIFT OF THE SPIRIT COMES BY FAITH —AND NOT BY LAW OR BY WORKS

Verse 1: "O foolish Galatians, who hath bewitched you, that ye should not obey the truth, before whose eyes Jesus Christ hath been evidently set forth, crucified among you?"

Paul is here referring to the preaching of the Gospel of grace which he himself had preached in Galatia. He preached Jesus Christ crucified . . . in fact, his message was singular:

"God forbid that I should glory, save in the cross of our Lord Jesus Christ . . . For I am determined not to know any thing among you, save Jesus Christ, and Him crucified" (Gal. 6:14; I Cor. 15:1–4).

Verse 2: "This only would I learn of you, Received ye the Spirit by the works of the Law, or by the hearing of faith?"

The believer receives the gift of the Holy Spirit when he is saved. When one is born again, the Holy Ghost immediately enters the heart (Rom. 8:8–9, I Cor. 6:19, Eph. 4:30, John 3:3, and John 3:5). The believers at Galatia knew what had happened in their lives. They knew the experience they had had, and Paul is asking them how it happened. Did the blessing they received come through Law-works, or by hearing and believing the Gospel of the grace of God?

The Galatians knew the answer, whether they admitted it or not. They knew that no person can be saved by turning over a new leaf, by doing the best he can, by practicing good works, or by joining the church. "FAITH COMETH BY HEARING, AND HEARING BY THE WORD OF GOD" (Rom. 10:17). Paul asked these people, "Did you receive the experience you enjoyed (until the legalizers came along) by working––or by hearing? By doing ––or by receiving? Through ritual––or through faith?" He seems to suggest this: "You Galatians know the answer!"

Verses 3 and 4: "Are ye so foolish? Having begun in the Spirit, are ye now made perfect by the flesh? Have ye suffered so many things in vain? if it be yet in vain."

There are tens of thousands of church members in America (and around the world) today who were saved by believing on the Lord Jesus Christ (putting their faith in the finished work of the Lamb of God), who are striving day by day to make themselves perfect in the flesh through the practice of religious dogmas, traditions of men, commandments of men, rules and regulations laid down by churches and denominations. They are seeking to perfect themselves through the energy of the flesh; but sooner or later they learn to their sad regret that the flesh is no good . . . God gave it up in the Garden. He provided redemption for the spirit, but to Adam Jehovah said, "Dust thou art, to dust thou shalt return." Later, Isaiah thundered out, "ALL OUR RIGHTEOUSNESSES ARE AS FILTHY RAGS!" (Isa. 64:6b).

Regardless of how much good you may try to do, regardless of how much money you give, regardless of how clean you live, regardless of how perfect you become in your own sight . . . everything good that you do, everything good that you are, adds up to no better than filthy rags in the sight of God Almighty. But by simple faith in the shed blood of Jesus Christ, you can instantaneously become as pure as the blood of the Lamb.

This is the way the Holy Spirit states it: "Though I speak with the tongues of men and of angels, and have not charity (love . . . Jesus), I am become as sounding brass, or a tinkling cymbal. And though I have the gift of prophecy, and understand all mysteries, and all knowledge; and though I have all faith, so that I could remove mountains, and have not charity (love . . . Jesus), I am nothing. And though I bestow all my goods to feed the poor, and though I give my body to be burned, and have not charity (love . . . Jesus), it profiteth me nothing" (I Cor. 13:1–3).

In other words, regardless of what I am, what I do, what I live or what I give, if I do not have the Lord Jesus Christ in my heart, then all of my living and giving adds up to one giant zero . . . one giant bundle of filthy rags. But in Christ, by faith in His finished work, I *now* am a son of God. I *now* am in Christ. I presently sit in heavenly places in Christ Jesus. I am dead––and my life is hid with Christ in God. I am justified by faith in His finished work––and to be justified in the sight of God is to be just as though I had never sinned. When Jehovah God looks at me, He sees the blood of Jesus that covers me . . . He does not see poor, helpless, Oliver Greene; He sees the precious blood of the Lamb of God. *"Hallelujah! What a Saviour! Who can take a poor, lost sinner——lift him from the miry clay and set him free!"*

"Come now, and let us reason together, saith the Lord: though your sins be as scarlet, they shall be as white as snow; though they be red like crimson, they shall be as wool" (Isa. 1:18).

Weary church member, frustrated religionist, cease your striving, enduring, working; this moment begin believing, trusting, resting . . . cast all your care upon Jesus. He is able to bear it . . . you are not!

Verse 5: "He therefore that ministereth to you the Spirit, and worketh miracles among you, doeth he it by the works of the Law, or by the hearing of faith?"

Paul does not name the person, nor intimate who it is, through which the Spirit is working miracles in Galatia. It is not important that we know the name. (One reason I know the Bible was written by God and not by man, is that many times when man would give names with honor and glory, the Spirit simply makes a statement without names.) Notice the words again: "He therefore that ministereth to you the Spirit, and worketh miracles among you, doeth he it by the works of the Law, or by the hearing of faith?" The point here is that the Spirit is the One who works miracles and who has the power to do the impossible . . . not Law-works or man's ability through attempting to keep the Law. Miracles are wrought by faith——not by works.

America does not need more theological institutions in which to train preachers how to stand in the pulpit, raise and lower their arms, and prepare great messages to be read on Sunday morning. America needs more ministers, pastors and evangelists who will lose themselves long enough with Jesus to acquire the kind of faith He had when He cast out the demon in the boy who fell into the fire and into the water. This boy's father had brought him to the disciples, but they could not cure him. When Jesus rebuked the demon, he immediately came out, and the young man was made perfectly whole. The disciples marveled and asked why they could not perform the miracle. Jesus told them, "This kind goeth not out but by prayer and fasting" (Matt. 17:14—21). Fasting is a lost art in the modern church. Instead of fasting, the average church can seat more people in the social hall than in the sanctuary. They have more soup suppers than they have prayer meetings. Fasting-and-praying is not practiced in most modern churches. Miracles of grace fall upon the people when great faith is exercised by spiritual leaders. Great faith can be acquired only by hearing the Word of God. The reason most preachers have so little faith is because they spend more time around the television and on the golf course than they spend alone with God studying His Word.

"So then, faith cometh by hearing, and hearing by the Word of God" (Rom. 10:17). Jesus said, "Have faith in God" (Mark 11:22).

PAUL DECLARES THAT ABRAHAM WAS SAVED EXACTLY AS WE ARE

Verses 6—9: "Even as Abraham believed God, and it was accounted to him for righteousness. Know ye therefore that they which are of faith, the same are the children of Abraham. And the Scripture, foreseeing that God would justify the heathen through faith, preached before the Gospel unto Abraham, saying, In thee shall all nations be blessed. So then they which be of faith are blessed with faithful Abraham."

The Jews honored Abraham very highly—and certainly they knew Abraham lived long before the Law of Moses. Therefore, Paul is pointing out to them the fact that Abraham was justified before Almighty God by faith. God spoke, Abraham heard; he believed—and God counted it to him as righteousness.

I think it would be time well spent to look briefly at the experience Abraham had with Jehovah God:

"Now the Lord had said unto Abram, Get thee out of thy country, and from thy kindred, and from thy father's house unto a land that I will shew thee: And I will make of thee a great nation, and I will bless thee, and make thy name great; and thou shalt be a blessing: And I will bless them that bless thee, and curse him that curseth thee: and in thee shall all families of the earth be blessed" (Gen. 12:1-3). Please note: The Lord spoke to Abraham. His message was, "Get thee out of thy country, from thy kindred and from thy father's house, unto a land I will show thee." Abraham did not see God—he HEARD God—and he believed God.

". . . I will show thee."

". . . I will make of thee a great nation."

". . . I will bless thee and make thy name great, and thou shalt be a blessing."

". . . I will bless them that bless thee, and curse him that curseth thee, and in thee shall all families of the earth be blessed."

Note: There are four "I will's":

1. "I will show thee."

2. "I will make thee."

3. I will bless thee."

4. "I will bless them that bless thee."

It will be a happy day in your life and in mine when we stop dead still and recognize the fact that every spiritual blessing, from the beginning to the end, comes only through God; and that we can receive God's blessings only by faith. God honors faith, and faith alone.

Verse 4 tells us what Abraham did after he heard the message of God: "SO ABRAM DEPARTED, AS THE LORD HAD SPOKEN UNTO HIM."

Abraham did exactly what the Lord God told him to do, exactly as the Lord told him to do it. He did not add to the Lord's message nor did he take from the message: "So ABRAM DEPARTED, AS THE LORD HAD SPOKEN UNTO HIM." But today our religious leaders have become so wise, and have learned so much, that they cannot afford to take this old Book literally. They must revise it, and then revise the revision, to make it fit their ideas and tickle the ears of the crowd to whom they preach on Sunday morning. But beloved, God is neither dead nor asleep. God keeps books. One day the books will be opened——and God pity the modern crowd who are butchering the Gospel just as surely as these Judaizers and legalizers butchered the message delivered by Paul——the message of salvation by grace through faith plus nothing.

In speaking to the Jews, his brethren in the flesh, Paul asked, "How was Abraham saved? How was father Abraham kept? Was he kept by the Law? Certainly not . . . for Abraham knew nothing of the Law. Abraham lived four hundred years before the Law was given!" (Gal. 3:17). I can almost see Paul as he looks straight into the faces of his Jewish brethren and asks the second time, "How

WAS our father Abraham saved and kept?" Then he answers his own question: "ABRAHAM BELIEVED GOD —and it was accounted to him for righteousness" (Gal. 3:6).

To the Romans Paul said, "ABRAHAM BELIEVED GOD, and it was accounted unto him for righteousness." Please note in both of these passages (Gal. 3:6 and Rom. 4:3) Paul said Abraham "BELIEVED GOD." Paul did not say "Abraham believed ABOUT God," or that he "believed IN God"; Paul said, "Abraham BELIEVED GOD!" There is a vast difference in believing *about God* and simply *believing* God. James 2:19 tells us, "The devils believe, and tremble." No one but a fool would say there is no God (Psalm 14:1). A man may believe a lot of wonderful things about God, and he may believe there IS a God——but unless he *believes God* he is just as lost as the heathen who has never heard about God.

What does it mean to believe God? The answer is found in Abraham's demonstration: God spoke to Abraham and simply commanded him to arise and leave his country and his father's house. God did not give him a roadmap, God did not tell him how many miles he should go, He did not tell him where to go; He simply told Abraham, "Get up and get out . . . and I will show thee!" God made Abraham a promise: He said, "I will bless you, I will make of you a great nation, I will bless everyone who blesses you and I will curse everyone who curses you." Abraham simply moved out on the Word of God . . . he *heard* God, he *believed* Him, and he *obeyed* Him. He had no roadmaps or blueprints. The only guarantee he had was God's promise. He believed God. To believe God is to accept His Word unconditionally; to trust His promise. To believe that God exists is not enough. To believe that God is good is not enough. To believe that God is holy is not enough.

"Verily, verily, I say unto you, He that heareth My word, and believeth on Him that sent Me, hath everlasting life" (John 5:24).

What did Abraham believe? He believed what God said . . . God spoke, Abraham listened, and he believed. God has spoken to you and to me . . . we have His written Word, the verbally inspired Word of God; and through that Word God tells us that He so loved us He gave Jesus to die for us (John 3:16). He tells us that He did not send Jesus into the world to condemn the world, but that through Him the world might be saved (John 3:17). God further instructs us that if we believe on Jesus we are not condemned; but if we do not believe, we are already condemned (John 3:18). He tells us that we are saved by grace, through faith, and that not of ourselves; it is the gift of God (Eph. 2:8). He tells us not to boast about works (Eph. 2:9). He tells us to believe on the Lord Jesus Christ, and we will be saved (Acts 16:31). God commands us to confess with our mouth the Lord Jesus, believe in our heart that God raised Him from the dead, and we shall surely be saved (Rom. 10:9). God tells us that whosoever shall call upon the name of the Lord shall be saved (Rom. 10:13). He tells us that saving faith comes by hearing, and hearing comes only by the Word of God (Rom. 10:17). So, if we will *read* the Word of God, *hear* the Word of God, and BELIEVE the Word of God, He will accept us "in the Beloved"—righteous, holy, pure, sinless, undefiled, without spot or wrinkle, and we will immediately become a member of the bride of Christ, the body of Christ, of which Jesus is the Head (Eph. 5:25–30).

God had promised Abraham that through him all the families of the earth would be blessed. Abraham had reached a ripe old age and so had Sarah——but God asked Abraham to believe the promise that even though he and his wife were both dead (from the standpoint of physical reproduction) He could miraculously and supernaturally give them a son.

"Now Abraham and Sarah were old and well stricken in age; and it ceased to be with Sarah after the manner of women" (Gen. 18:11). In the letter to the Hebrews, Paul tells us, "Through faith also Sara herself received strength to conceive seed, and was delivered of a child when she was past age, because she judged Him faithful who had promised" (Heb. 11:11). What was true of Sarah was also true of Abraham. He had passed the years of fertility and was dead (from the standpoint of being able to produce children through natural avenues of reproduction). But we read, "(Abraham) who against hope *believed in hope*, that he (Abraham) might become the father of many nations; according to that which was spoken, So shall thy seed be. And being not weak in faith, he considered not his own body now dead, when he was about an hundred years old, neither yet the deadness of Sarah's womb: he staggered not at the promise of God through unbelief; but was strong in faith, giving glory to God; and being fully persuaded that, what He had promised, HE WAS ABLE ALSO TO PERFORM. And therefore it was imputed to him for righteousness" (Rom. 4:18—22).

Here is the record: Abraham's body was dead, Sarah's body was dead, and it was imperative that God work a miracle or there could be no child through which all families of the earth could be blessed; but God had promised, and Abraham believed God. He believed that God was able to do what He had promised, even if it took a miracle. The birth of Isaac was as great a miracle as the birth of the Lord Jesus. Isaac was a type of the Lord Jesus——and through the seed of Abraham, in the fulness of time, Jesus was born . . . born of a woman, born under the Law, to redeem them that were under the Law (Gal. 4:4).

What was true in Abraham's day is true in our day. Salvation, justification, redemption . . . any blessing we receive from God must of necessity become ours through believing God (or, by faith). If we *believe* God, we have faith IN God.

"If we receive the witness of men, the witness of God is greater: for this is the witness of God which He hath testified of His Son. He that believeth on the Son of God hath the witness in himself: HE THAT BELIEVETH NOT GOD HATH MADE HIM A LIAR; because he believeth not the record that God gave of His Son"(I John 5:9—10).

Certainly these verses are crystal-clear, easily understood. Any person who will believe God concerning Jesus Christ will have the witness of God in his heart; but any person who hears the Gospel story of the death, burial, and resurrection of Jesus Christ and refuses to believe it, makes God a liar. To hear the Gospel story and refuse to believe it is to label God a liar——there are no "if's, and's or maybe's" about it. It is clearly stated in the Scripture just quoted. God has no other plan, there is no other way, God has provided no other way because no other way COULD be provided. It had to be Jesus. It was imperative that He die. If He had not died, we would all die and burn in hell! Jesus is the Way, the Truth and the Life. He is the straight gate, He is the one door, He is the author and the finisher of our faith. Jesus IS our salvation.

"Now it was not written for his sake alone, that it was imputed to him; But for us also, to whom it shall be imputed, if we believe on Him that raised up Jesus our Lord from the dead; who was delivered for our offences, and was raised again for our justification" (Rom. 4:23–25). Therefore, ". . . If thou shalt confess with thy mouth the Lord Jesus, and shalt believe in thine heart that God hath raised Him from the dead, thou shalt be saved. For with the heart man believeth unto righteousness; and with the mouth confession is made unto salvation" (Rom. 10:9–10).

Verse 10: "For as many as are of the works of the Law are under the curse: for it is written, Cursed is every one that continueth not in all things which are written in the book of the Law to do them."

The main words in this verse are, "ALL THINGS." If the sinner is to be justified by Law-works, let that sinner know that he must obey the Law (all of it) perfectly . . . in every minute detail. There can no part of it be broken . . . he must obey "all things" that are written in the Law, and he must obey them all of his life . . . "FOR WHOSOEVER SHALL KEEP THE WHOLE LAW, AND YET OFFEND IN ONE POINT, HE IS GUILTY OF ALL" (James 2:10). Certainly anyone who is reasonable would readily agree that salvation through this method would be utterly impossible. How could an imperfect man keep God's perfect, holy Law, without breaking one jot or one tittle? Therefore, unless we are saved by God's grace (God's unmerited favor) through faith plus nothing, then face it––there is no salvation for us! Salvation must be of the Lord, totally and entirely of the Lord, entirely apart from man. Everything that man has ever touched, he has corrupted. God is not the author of corruption––God is holy, and all of His works are holy. He accepts nothing less than holiness: "Without holiness no man shall see God."

In verse 11 Paul thunders out: "But that no man is justified by the Law in the sight of God, it is evident:

for, THE JUST SHALL LIVE BY FAITH."

The last part of that verse is recorded in God's holy Word no less than four times:
1. "The just shall live by his faith" (Habakkuk 2:4).
2. "The just shall live by faith" (Romans 1:17).
3. "The just shall live by faith" (Galatians 3:11).
4. "Now the just shall live by faith" (Hebrews 10:38).

Habakkuk states the fact that the man who humbles himself before God, the man who trusts in God, the man who looks to God, the man who leans upon God, is the man who is blessed by God. There may be woes all around, judgments without, vexation and heartbreak within, fears beside, famine before, disaster behind—but in spite of it all, the man who lives with God lives through it all in peace! Please read carefully Habakkuk 3:17–19.

In his letter to the believers at Rome, Paul emphasizes again and again that the Gospel reveals the righteousness of faith . . . the righteousness which God alone imputed to faith. Christ, who is the righteousness of God, is put to the account of faith. Please read carefully Romans 4:3, 5, 6, 9, 11, 13, and 22. Also read Romans 10:6–10. Also Galatians 3:6. Righteousness is an objective state in which man is placed by the divine act of a holy God.

According to the Apostle Paul, the righteousness of God embraces two bestowals of grace. The recipient of God's marvelous grace stands before God as if he had never committed any evil, as if he had always accomplished all the good God could expect from him. Face it: God's grace provides for the sinner, and brings to the sinner God's holiness—because it was the blood of God that flowed through the veins of Jesus. God purchased the church with His own blood. To the Romans, Paul stated: "I am not ashamed of the Gospel of Christ: for it is the power of God unto salvation to every one that believeth; to the Jew first, and also to the Greek. For therein is the righteousness of God revealed from faith to faith: as it is written, THE JUST SHALL LIVE BY FAITH" (Rom. 1:16—17).

The meaning of the statement "from faith to faith" is not from one degree of faith to another; but what Paul is pointing out here is the fact that God blesses the believer on the *principle* of faith. God offers justification to the unbeliever on the ground of faith, not on the ground of works. We are justified by faith, and "the justified" shall live on the principle of faith——or, BY faith, in the finished work of the Lord Jesus.

Writing to the saints in Galatia, Paul contrasts faith and Christ with Law and works. The words for "faith" in the Greek occur twenty-seven times in Galatians. Faith expresses itself in confidence toward God. Faith looks away from self to God. Faith is committal to God. Faith is separation from self to *Him*self. Faith is communion with God, content to rest in the promises laid down in His precious Word.

There is no way around it, there is no need to argue: According to the teachings of the Word of God and the preaching of the minister ordained of God and given to the Gentiles, we are *saved* by faith, we are *kept* by faith, we are *rewarded* according to our faith——and every blessing received from Almighty God must be accepted by faith. Every work performed that will bring reward at the end of life's journey must be a work of faith. We read, "Whatsoever is not of faith is sin" (Rom. 14:23b).

Verse 12: "And the Law is not of faith: but, The man that doeth them shall live in them." What Paul is setting forth here is the fact that it is a question of *doing* or *believing*. He quotes here from Leviticus 18:5. What he is saying is simply this: If we seek salvation by the Law, then of necessity we must do all that the Law requires because God accepts nothing less than perfection in holiness, and certainly it is impossible for any finite person to keep the holy Law of an infinite God. The Law was not given to save anyone. The Law is a schoolmaster; by the Law is the knowledge of sin. By the deeds of the Law there shall be no flesh justified. How can a sinner perfectly obey the Law of God? The Gospel (the Good News) says––not "DO and live"–– but "BELIEVE and live!" After we are born again, we work, we do, we live, we sacrifice . . . but we do these things because we love Jesus––not to merit His love or His mercy. We work for Jesus because we love Him. We serve Him because of deep appreciation in our hearts for the salvation He so graciously provided and so freely gives when we believe on His precious name. God help us not to be so foolish as to think we can please God in the flesh. Only ONE ever heard God say, "This is my beloved Son, *in whom I am well pleased*!" Those words were spoken by God the Father, of the Lord Jesus when He was baptized, and again on the Mount of Transfiguration. The only way you and I can please God the Father is to believe on His Son, the Lord Jesus Christ; and when we believe on the Lord Jesus Christ we are "accepted in the Beloved," our names are written in the Lamb's Book of Life, we are placed in the body of Christ through the baptism of the Holy Spirit (I Cor. 12:12–13). We are sealed by the precious Holy Ghost until the day of redemption (Eph. 4:30). We are led by the Holy Spirit into the paths of right living (Rom. 8:14; Psalm 23). Therefore, if you, precious friend, want to be in that number when the saints go marching in, it is absolutely imperative that you set yourself aside, recognize the fact that you are totally depraved, hopelessly lost, past redemption so far as your own effort and merit is concerned. You must recognize that you are dead in trespasses and in sin, and by faith literally fling yourself at the feet of Jesus. Look up into His face with the eye of faith, reach out with the *hand* of faith, and receive the gift of God . . . Jesus Christ, His only begotten Son: "As many as received Him, to them gave He power to become the sons of God, even to them that believe on His name: which were born, not of blood, nor of the flesh, nor of the will of man, but of God" (John 1:12–13).

CHRIST HAS BORNE FOR US THE CURSE OF THE LAW, THAT WE IN HIM MIGHT HAVE THE BLESSING OF FAITH

Verse 13: "Christ hath redeemed us from the curse of the Law, being made a curse for us: for it is written, Cursed is every one that hangeth on a tree."

Paul is quoting from Deuteronomy: "And if a man have committed a sin worthy of death, and he be to be put to death, and thou hang him on a tree: his body shall not remain all night upon the tree, but thou shalt in any wise bury him that day; (for he that is hanged is accursed of God;) that thy land be not defiled, which the Lord thy God giveth thee for an inheritance" (Deut. 21:22–23).

In Deuteronomy 13:8–11 we learn that the Jewish method of executing criminals was not by hanging. They *stoned* the one condemned to die. However, if they cared to bring extra shame on the criminal they hung his body on a tree, and the criminals who were hung on a tree were cursed by the Law. (Read Acts 5:30 and Acts 10:39.) Jehovah God brought it to pass that the death of Jesus would be on a tree. (The cross is symbolic of a tree.) God allowed this in order to fulfill the prophecy of the curse Jesus became for us. Jesus came into the world to fulfill the Law and the prophets (Matt. 5:17), and He went all the way. He became "obedient unto death," but that is not all: "EVEN THE DEATH OF THE CROSS!" (Phil. 2:8). Jesus willingly laid down His life, He died voluntarily, He was not forced to die and there was no compulsion concerning His humiliation and suffering on a tree . . . it was of His own choosing, because He came to fulfill every demand of the holy God who was His Father.

During the days of Jesus, the Romans regarded crucifixion as entirely too shameful and disgraceful for a Roman citizen. They refused to allow a Roman citizen to be hanged. The Jews, too, looked upon crucifixion as very shameful——but they wanted to heap upon Jesus all the shame and disgrace possible. They referred to Him as "the Hanged One." In the early days of Christianity, the Jews called the Christians "worshippers of the Hanged One." The cross with its shame is a stumbling block to the flesh. Proud flesh recoils at the thought of a bloody salvation, purchased by the death of a man on a shameful cross! But Jesus died a shameful death——even the death of the cross——that you and I might be delivered from shame, disgrace and damnation. The natural man does not receive the cross with all of its shame and suffering, simply because to the natural man it is foolishness. Please read I Corinthians 1:18.

May I ask the question: Whom did Christ redeem from the curse of the Law, and for whom did the Lord Jesus become so great a curse?

The first part of verse 13 reads, "Christ hath redeemed US from the curse of the Law." Please note: "US." Great Bible scholars agree that the "US" applies solely, entirely, and ONLY to the Jews. The Jews were under the curse of Galatians 3:10, the Jews were the people under the Law of Moses. "When the fulness of the time was come, God sent forth His Son, made of a woman, made under the Law, to redeem them that were under the Law . . ." (Gal. 4:4—5a). Gentiles have never been under Law. We are not under Law today, nor will we ever be. The Law was given by Jehovah God to the nation Israel, of which the tribe of Judah was a part (and the Jews came from Judah). So Jesus was made a curse for His brethren in the flesh, that they might become the sons of God by exercising faith. They could receive the blessing of Abraham (justification by faith) if they would only believe on the Lord Jesus Christ; but of course the greater part of the Jews refused to accept Jesus as the Lamb of God, the Saviour of sinners. Rather, they looked upon Him as the despised Nazarene, born of fornication.

It is very clear in the New Testament that the Gentiles were never under Law. Read Romans 2:14. It is crystal clear that the Law was "the middle wall of partition" dividing the Jews from the Gentiles . . . and vice versa. Please read carefully Ephesians 2:13—18.

The ministers and religionists who would put us under Law, the ministers who would command their parishioners to keep the Law and practice the rituals of the Law, are wrongly dividing the Word of Truth . . . they are not rightly dividing God's precious Word and they will suffer severely for it in the day of judgment.

Verse 14: "That the blessing of Abraham might come on the Gentiles through Jesus Christ; that we might receive the promise of the Spirit through faith."

By the grace of God, Paul is attempting to show to the Jews that they were being shut out from the blessing, by the very Law in which they gloried. If that be true,

Gentiles certainly could not hope to obtain the blessing of God by putting themselves under the Law which could not bless the Jews! However, if the Jews could receive the blessing by faith in the death of Jesus Christ, by exercising faith in His finished work, then on the same grounds Gentiles also could receive the blessings provided by God——the blessings of faithful Abraham.

Writing to the believers at Corinth, Paul points out that Christ, who knew no sin, was made sin for us, that we in Him might be made the righteousness of God (II Cor. 5:21). Certainly it is exceedingly precious and blessed to know that Jesus was made sin for us. He knew no sin, but He took our sin and nailed it to His cross. It is also precious to learn here that He was also made a curse for us. I like to put it in these words: "What a holy God commands and demands, the same holy God *provides* in the finished work of the Lord Jesus." Jesus satisfied every demand of God the Father, He fulfilled every minute detail of the Law and of the prophets. We are complete in Jesus, because Jesus lived completeness in the flesh, He lived pure holiness in the flesh . . . not one aught was ever brought against Jesus.

In II Corinthians 5:21, Paul puts himself with all believers. He is not contrasting between believers and Jews, nor between Gentiles and Jews. Consequently the "we" in that verse includes ALL——*everyone*. But in Galatians 3:13 the "US" refers exclusively to the Jews. The reason I am so dogmatic in this statement is because a bit later Paul refers particularly and distinctly to the Gentiles: ". . . that the blessing of Abraham might come on the Gentiles through Jesus Christ." Immediately following, Paul puts all believers in one group: "THAT WE MIGHT RECEIVE THE PROMISE OF THE SPIRIT THROUGH FAITH."

In Galatians 3:13, the "US" is very emphatic! In

verse 14, the "WE" is not at all emphatic, but is used by Paul in a general way, referring to all believers, whether in that day or in our day.

I wonder why some ministers who put their parishioners under Law do not speak from the text, "AS MANY AS ARE OF THE WORKS OF THE LAW ARE UNDER THE CURSE!" If you will carefully read Deuteronomy 27 and 28, you will see the promised blessings of Jehovah upon Israel *if they obeyed God*. The blessings were conditioned upon Israel's obedience: "If thou shalt . . . do His commandments . . . all these blessings shall come on thee" (Deut. 38:1—2). Of course, we are on this side of the command, and these dear people have long since gone on to their reward; but we know they did not obey. They did everything BUT obey, and the judgment of God fell heavily upon them. Any person or nation who takes the Legal ground for receiving blessings from Almighty God will receive only curses, because the blessings of God come by faith——not by works, not by Law——but by faith in the finished work of the Lord Jesus Christ. The person who will acknowledge the Law's curse because of sin, and the fact that the Law was not given to save us from the curse (but to make us AWARE OF it), can then by grace through faith become a child of God. "Christ hath redeemed us from the curse of the Law, being made a curse for us." Jesus was not just "accursed," He was made "A CURSE." Jesus fully identified Himself with the curse. He took the curse . . . took our sin . . . and nailed it to His cross; therefore those of us who have accepted the grace of God are completely delivered from the curse—yea, we are delivered from the Law, and we live by faith! It was imperative for God to move the curse out of the way, in order that the blessing might come to Jews and Gentiles alike. The Gospel was first to the Jew and then to the Gentile. The cup of grace was first presented to the Jew——but the cup overflowed and the blessings spilled over onto the Gentiles. Thank God, today there is no "middle wall of partition"——but Jesus Christ saves to the uttermost ALL who will come to God by Him! Jesus was made a curse for us: "It is written, Cursed is everyone that hangeth on a tree . . . that the BLESSING OF ABRAHAM MIGHT COME ON THE GENTILES THROUGH JESUS CHRIST." Thank God for the marvelous blessing God purchased for the Gentiles through the death of Jesus, that we might receive the promise of the Spirit through faith. I thank God that it is not by might, it is not by power, it is not by works, it is not by "doing," it is not by giving——nor is it by living; *it is by faith*. God honors faith——childlike faith——in the finished work of the Lord Jesus. Jesus said, "Except ye be converted, and become as little children, ye shall not enter into the kingdom of heaven" (Matt. 18:3).

Before leaving this section, let me emphasize (I cannot *over*emphasize) the fact that we are not under Law. Salvation is totally and entirely apart from Law:

"For what the Law could not do, in that it was weak through the flesh, God sending His own Son in the likeness of sinful flesh, and for sin, condemned sin in the flesh: That the righteousness of the Law might be fulfilled in us, who walk not after the flesh, but after the Spirit" (Rom. 8:3–4). It is one thing to read the Scripture——it is another to study. So——shall we stop for a moment and *study*? Please notice: "THAT THE RIGHTEOUSNESS OF THE LAW MIGHT BE FULFILLED IN US." The Scripture does not say, "That the righteousness of the Law might be fulfilled BY us." The Scripture says, "That the righteousness of the Law might be fulfilled IN us." Certainly the Lord Jesus in our heart is the One who fulfills the righteousness of the Law, because He came "not to destroy the Law, but to fulfill the Law" (Matt. 5:17). Therefore, it is "Christ in you, the hope of glory"; and if Jesus is not in you, if you have not been born into the family of God by the power of the Word and the Spirit (John 3:1–7), then you cannot and will not fulfill the righteousness of the Law. It is absolutely impossible for the natural man to live the righteousness of the Law; but Christ lives in us. So—— we could not fulfill the Law, we could not keep the Law (no man save Jesus ever kept it), but . . . thank God, the righteousness of the Law which we could not attain is ours when we possess the Lord Jesus Christ.

Let me again remind you:

"As many as are of the works of the Law are under the curse: for it is written, Cursed is every one that continueth not in all things which are written in the book of the Law to do them" (Gal. 3:10). Here we see what the Law demands: It demands that one continue "in all things which are written in the book of the Law, to do them." Therefore, we are hopeless, helpless, hell-bound and condemned unless we can find One who is greater, One who is holier, One who is mightier than we. *That One is Jesus.*

"Christ hath redeemed us from the curse of the Law, being made a curse for us: for it is written, Cursed is every one that hangeth on a tree" (Gal. 3:13). Jesus took our place, He died for us. Therefore we are delivered from the Law (Rom. 7:6). The Law cannot condemn us twice. We were condemned——but Jesus took our condemnation; and when we receive Jesus we are through with the Law forever. The Law has no power over a believer. Christ is our Head, our Saviour, our Keeper, and our salvation . . . Jesus fulfilled every jot and every tittle of the Law. Therefore the believer is through with the Law forever when he abides in Christ by faith. The believer is dead to the Law (Gal. 2:19). The believer is free from the Law (Rom. 8:2). What a wonderful position! Believers are positionally righteous in Christ before God!

THE ABRAHAMIC AND THE MOSAIC COVENANTS

In chapter three, verses 15 through 25, we study about these two covenants:

Verse 15: "Brethren, I speak after the manner of men; Though it be but a man's covenant, yet if it be confirmed, no man disannulleth or addeth thereto."

In God's economy even a covenant between two men (when such covenant has been confirmed, signed, sealed, and recorded) is binding upon both parties, neither of whom has the right to make any change in the agreement. Certainly a covenant between God and man is more important than any contract between two men could be. God's covenant with faithful Abraham has been confirmed, and God will not set it aside. God will not change it or break it until every promise in it has been completely fulfilled.

Verse 16: "Now to Abraham and his seed were the promises made. He saith not, And to seeds, as of many; BUT AS OF ONE, AND TO THY SEED, WHICH IS CHRIST." I want you to carefully note here that the covenant referred to was between God on the one hand, and two men on the other. The two men were Abraham and Christ. The language is self-explanatory and to the point. The covenant was not to Abraham and his natural seed of the flesh——the children of Israel in general; nor was it to his heavenly seed in the church of the living God——believers in general. THE PROMISE WAS MADE TO ABRAHAM'S SEED (singular) . . . CHRIST, THE SEED OF THE WOMAN, WHO WOULD BRUISE THE HEAD OF THE SERPENT.

The devil did everything in his ungodly power to frustrate the plan and the program of God, and to corrupt the seed. There are many chapters in the Old Testament that vividly tell the story; but in spite of all Satan did, Jesus came—the Seed of the woman, conceived of the Holy Ghost. He came to make good every promise God had made to the faithful.

Verse 17: "And this I say, that the covenant, that was confirmed before of God in Christ, the Law, which was four hundred and thirty years after, cannot disannul, that it should make the promise of none effect."

The covenant God made with Abraham was unconditional—it could not be broken. Since the promises of God to Abraham have not yet been fulfilled, it stands to reason that the Abrahamic covenant could not be set aside by the Law given to Moses on Mount Sinai. You may rest assured that the Law did not set aside the covenant between God and Abraham.

Verse 18: "For if the inheritance be of the Law, it is no more of promise: but God gave it to Abraham by promise."

God's promises in the Abrahamic Covenant were promises based upon pure grace; there were no conditions attached to them. The fulfillment of the promises did not depend upon anything Abraham did or did not do, nor upon anything his *seed* did or promised to do. On the other hand, the Law of Moses made ALL of its promises conditional—that is, if Israel practiced obedience, then God granted the promise.

God uses the word "IF" for the first time in Exodus 19:5, in preparation for the giving of the Law. God said, "IF ye will obey my voice indeed, and keep my covenant, then ye shall be a peculiar treasure unto me above all people . . . ."

The people answered Jehovah by saying, "ALL THAT THE LORD HATH SPOKEN WE WILL DO" (Ex. 19:8). But if you will read the history of Israel, you will find that instead of doing everything Jehovah commanded, they did just the opposite! Time after time Jehovah God chastened Israel severely. This was entirely different from the covenant God made with Abraham. Abraham made no promise to God––either for himself or for his seed after him. All the promises were made by God, and carried with them no conditions whatsoever! Study carefully the Abrahamic Covenant and you will see that what I have just said is one hundred percent correct.

WHY, THEN, WAS THE LAW GIVEN?

Verse 19: "Wherefore than serveth the Law? It was added because of transgressions, till the seed should come to whom the promise was made; and it was ordained by angels in the hand of a mediator."

The question, "Wherefore then serveth the Law?" is a natural question in view of the statements Paul made in the preceding verses. Paul knew the question would be brought up, so he answered it before it was asked. In the first three chapters of Galatians, under the inspiration of the Holy Ghost, Paul proved that the Law of Moses was not given to save man, to make man righteous, nor to justify man. On the contrary, the Law was given to condemn the sinner, in order that he might realize his need for the Grace of God. Paul showed beyond a shadow of a doubt that the death of Christ is the final argument that salvation cannot come by the Law. *"If righteousness come by the Law, then Christ is dead in vain!"*

The minister who preaches salvation by the Law,

or salvation by grace *plus* Law, denies the finished work of Christ. He also denies the necessity of the death of the Lord Jesus Christ. The Law cannot save, the Law cannot sanctify, the Law cannot redeem. The Law cannot make man better. All the Law could do was to show man how exceeding sinful he was, and how hopeless he stood before God without the *Grace of God*.

Paul preached to the Galatians that the Law could neither justify, sanctify, nor satisfy the sinner. He knew they would ask, "Wherefore then serveth the Law? What is the Law for? Why did God give it, if the Law cannot save a man or keep him saved?" Paul answers: "(The Law) was added because of transgressions, till the seed should come." In this brief verse we see clearly that the Law did have a specific and definite *beginning* . . . "IT WAS ADDED" . . . it was added to something that existed before the Law came.

Then too, the Law had a definite *purpose*. God does not do anything unless He does it for a specific reason, a specific purpose. The Law was added "BECAUSE OF TRANSGRESSIONS." The Law was added *to reveal the true nature* of unregenerate man. The Law had an *end*, just as truly as it had a beginning: "It was added TILL THE SEED SHOULD COME." When the Seed came (THE LORD JESUS) the Law came to an end. "Christ is the end of the Law for righteousness to everyone that believeth" (Rom. 10:4). There is no place in all the Word of God where the purpose of the Law is more clearly set forth than in the verse we have just studied.

I can almost hear someone saying, "Mr. Greene, the statement 'the Law was added because of transgression until the seed should come' was made concerning the ceremonial laws, and not the Ten Commandments!" There is no doubt in my mind that such a statement will be made by many who will read these lines; but let me hasten to say that Paul (in speaking of the Law) was not speaking of the ceremonial laws, nor of the dietary laws, the laws of sacrifice nor of the laws of the land. Paul was speaking of THE WHOLE LAW, and he was speaking in particular of the Ten Commandments! Paul was speaking of the Law which cursed the sinner. He was speaking of God's holy Law. Some men are very clever when they make distinction between the Law of Moses (so called) and the Law of God; but these clever religionists do not have Scripture to back up their argument. Their doctrine is self-invented, and it is a dogma of man, not of Bible doctrine.

If the Law was added, just when did the Law have its beginning? The answer is found in John 1:17: "FOR THE LAW WAS GIVEN BY MOSES, but grace and truth came by Jesus Christ." Could anything be more plainly stated? Could anything be more understandable? The Law——ALL of the Law——was given to a specific people at a specific time. The Law was given to Israel, delivered by Moses exactly as he received it from Almighty God on Mount Sinai.

The last part of Galatians 3:19 tells us, ". . . till the seed should come to whom the promise was made; and it was ordained by angels in THE HAND OF A MEDIATOR."

The mediator here spoken of was Moses, the Lawgiver. Not even Israel knew anything about Law until God dictated the Ten Commandments to Moses on Mount Sinai. From Adam to Moses——a period of more than two thousand years——there were no Ten Commandments. "For until the Law sin was in the world: but sin is not imputed when there is no Law" (Rom. 5:13). Man knew nothing of the written Law of God until God gave that

Law to Moses on the Mount; but before the Law came, the grace of God was displayed for more than two thousand years. Adam lived under the grace of God——certainly God showed unmerited favor toward Adam in the Garden of Eden. Noah lived in a generation of wicked men——but *he found grace in the eyes of the Lord*: "By faith Noah, being warned of God of things not seen as yet, moved with fear, prepared an ark to the saving of his house; by the which he condemned the world, and became heir of the righteousness which is by faith" (Heb. 11:7). Abraham lived under the grace of God—— he believed God, and it was counted unto him for righteousness. God dealt in grace two thousand years before the Law of Moses, and God dealt in grace during the *time* of the Law of Moses. He is *still* dealing in grace. The Gospel is good news, and that Gospel was preached to Abraham. The good news of the Gospel is that by grace, hell-deserving sinners can become sons of God, heirs of God, and joint-heirs with Christ. The Gospel is the good news that the sinner can be saved *by* grace, *through* faith, plus nothing! The Law is NOT good news to the sinner. The Law is bad news for the transgressor, because it condemns him and shows him how wicked he is. The Law accuses the sinner and declares him accursed and condemned. The Law demands the death of the sinner: "The soul that sinneth, it shall die!" (Ezek. 18:4). "The wages of sin is death" (Rom. 6:23). The *bad news* of the Law was added to the *good news* of God's grace. In other words, it was placed alongside God's grace to show the sinner how exceeding sinful sin is. The Law did not take the place of the grace of God ——and it was not given to be mixed with grace. It was not intended to supplement the Grace of God. It was added (or, as the original Greek states, it was "placed alongside" God's grace). Therefore the Law was added (or placed alongside the Gospel of grace) to reveal to the sinner his true character, and his great need of the grace of God. By the works of the Law no one has ever been saved, nor ever will be saved. By the deeds of the Law there shall be no flesh justified in His sight (Rom. 3:20).

Notice these words: "Is the Law then against the promises (the promises of the Gospel) of God? God forbid: for if there had been a law given which could have given life, verily righteousness should have been by the Law. But the Scripture hath concluded all under sin, that the promise by faith of Jesus Christ might be given to them that BELIEVE" (Gal. 3:21–22).

God is love. God has no pleasure in the death of the wicked. God's judgment and fiery indignation is truly "HIS STRANGE WORK" (Isaiah 28:21). According to Micah 7:18, the Lord God Almighty is a God who "DELIGHTETH IN MERCY." God delights in mercy, and He has no pleasure in the death of the wicked; but He cannot *acquit* the wicked, nor can He overlook sin. God forgives sin for Jesus' sake when the sinner exercises faith in the shed blood of His cross.

Verses 19b and 20: ". . . IN THE HAND OF A MEDIATOR. Now a mediator is not a mediator of one, but God is one."

In the covenant between God and Abraham, there was only one party who made promises (or who was under obligation). That one party was Almighty God. Abraham made no promises to God, therefore there was no need for a mediator between God and Abraham. On the other hand, the covenant of Sinai was a conditional covenant. God made the promises, but His promises were conditional. The people Israel must obey and follow God's command; therefore, a mediator between God and man was needed. It is true that the Lord Jesus Christ is declared in the New Testament as the ONE mediator between God and man (I Tim. 2:5), but Jesus is not a mediator separating two parties to a covenant, as Moses did. Jesus is One in whom the two parties (God and man) are united to become one in body.

When we are born again by faith in the shed blood of the Lord Jesus, we actually become a member of His body—bone of His bone and flesh of His flesh (Eph. 5:30). Believers are dead and their lives are hid with Christ in God (Col. 3:3).

"For the Law was given by Moses, but grace and truth came by Jesus Christ" (John 1:17). Here we see the two mediators—Moses, during the Dispensation of the Law, and Jesus, who is now the one Mediator between God and man during this Dispensation of Grace.

"I (Moses) stood between the Lord and you at that time, to shew you the word of the Lord: for ye were afraid by reason of the fire, and went not up into the mount" (Deut. 5:5).

"There is one God, and *one Mediator* between God and men, the man Christ Jesus" (I Tim. 2:5).

Verse 21: "Is the Law then against the promises of God? God forbid: for if there had been a law given which could have given life, verily righteousness should have been by the Law."

Paul raises another question: "Is the Law then against the promises of God?" In the same breath, he answers the question: "God forbid!"

The question is simply this: Is the Law which involves a mediator (Moses) contrary to the promises of God which are without a mediator, which promises rest entirely upon God for their fulfillment? The answer to that question, of course, is "God forbid!"

Paul clearly states the fact that if life can come through the Law, if there had been a Law given that could bring life, then certainly righteousness would have come by the Law and there would have been no need for the horrible death of Jesus on the cross. I believe anyone who wants to be reasonable can understand the last part of verse 21. What Paul is saying is simply this: It was impossible for God to give a law that could produce life. God is holy, He cannot look upon sin, He cannot acquit the wicked. Because of God's holiness, He *demands* holiness: "Without holiness no man shall see God." Therefore it was impossible for a holy God to give to unholy men a law that would make them holy. The holy Law of a holy God could not make men better, but could only show them how sinful they really are. Therefore it was imperative that Jesus take a body, and in that body fulfill every jot and every tittle of God's holy Law in order that we in Christ might become the righteousness of God which is by faith.

It is true that the Law promises life to whosoever should perfectly obey it——but who on this earth except Jesus Christ ever perfectly obeyed God's holy Law? Let the Book answer: "THERE IS NOT A JUST MAN UPON THE EARTH THAT DOETH GOOD AND SINNETH NOT." Again, "ALL HAVE SINNED AND COME SHORT OF THE GLORY OF GOD!" "ALL WE LIKE SHEEP HAVE GONE ASTRAY, And the Lord hath laid on Him (Jesus) the iniquity of us all." Again we read, "There is none righteous . . . no, not one." And finally we hear the Holy Spirit speaking through John, "If we say we have no sin, we make God a liar!" I ask, in the name of all that is high and holy, What man would dare suggest that he could live a life worthy of the salvation given by a holy God? Salvation comes only through the shed blood of the Lamb of God. (Study carefully Romans 10:5–10.)

Verse 22: "But the Scripture hath concluded all under sin, that the promise by faith of Jesus Christ might be given to them that believe."

Who would dare argue with the Word of God? The Scriptures declare that ALL are under sin . . . ALL are in the same category . . . "that the promise by faith of Jesus Christ might be given to them THAT BELIEVE." Faith and believing cannot be separated . . . they are Siamese twins so far as spiritual matters are concerned. If we believe in Jesus we have faith in Him; if we have faith in Jesus we believe in Him. The only way any person has ever been saved (or ever *will* be saved) is by believing the Word of the Living God. "Faith comes by hearing, and hearing by the Word of God" (Rom. 10:17). We should remember that the Scriptures had not been written in Abraham's time. The Scriptures began to be written about the time the Law was given. The first five books, often referred to as the Books of Moses, were written by the mediator of the Law Covenant . . . and of course that was Moses. Thank God for the written Word today! Thank God for Galatians 5:1. We enjoy ". . . the liberty wherewith Christ hath made us free!"

Verse 23: "But before faith came, we were kept under the Law, shut up unto the faith which should afterwards be revealed."

In this verse we again have the words "shut up." Greek scholars tell us this verse should read, "But before faith came, we were kept in ward (in jail) under the Law, shut up unto the faith which should afterwards be revealed."

Of course, the people who were shut up (or in jail)

were the people of Israel to whom the Law was given. The Scripture states, "We know that what things soever the Law saith, it saith to them who are under the Law" (Rom. 3:19). On the other hand, Gentiles are similarly condemned; for though they (Gentiles) do not have the Law, they "are a law unto themselves: which shew the work of the Law written in their hearts, their conscience also bearing witness, and their thoughts the mean while accusing or else excusing one another" (Rom. 2:14b—15).

"FOR WHEN THE GENTILES WHICH HAVE NOT THE LAW . . . ." Could anything be more clearly stated? Could it be made plainer? I referred to the Council in Acts 15 a little earlier in this message. The big question *there* was whether or not the Gentiles were under the Law of Moses. After the apostles deliberated and discussed the question as to whether or not believers are under Law, they sent back this message to the Gentile Christians at Antioch: "Forasmuch as we have heard, that certain which went out from us have troubled you with words, subverting your souls, saying, Ye must be circumcised, and keep the Law: to whom we gave no such commandment" (Acts 15:24). In the same chapter Peter accuses the legalizers of "putting a yoke" on the shoulders of God's people, which no man could bear (or, which could not be borne by man). "Now therefore why tempt ye God, to put a yoke upon the neck of the disciples, which neither our fathers nor we were able to bear? BUT WE BELIEVE THAT THROUGH THE GRACE OF THE LORD JESUS CHRIST WE SHALL BE SAVED, EVEN AS THEY!" (Acts 15:10—11).

God gave His holy Law to one nation (Israel) as a demonstration of man's inability to save himself by keeping that Law:

"Now we know that what things soever the Law

saith, it saith to them who are under the Law: that every mouth may be stopped, and all the world may become guilty before God. Therefore by the deeds of the Law there shall no flesh be justified in His sight: FOR BY THE LAW IS THE KNOWLEDGE OF SIN" (Rom. 3:19—20).

The Word of God clearly defines the reason for giving of the Law: The Law was given to Israel to stop the mouths of all men forever . . . that is, all men who teach salvation by Law . . . or by grace plus Law . . . or by grace plus Law-works. For more than fifteen hundred years God gave Israel the opportunity to prove that man cannot keep the Law. God did not need proof . . . He knew that man would sadly fail. Man should need no further proof. If during the course of fifteen hundred years, Israel could not keep the Law (they broke every Law God ever gave them), we should face the fact that no one can be saved by keeping the Law. All must be saved by faith, and faith alone, without the deeds of the Law, without the deeds of the flesh. The Word of God clearly points out, "By the Law is the knowledge of sin." The Word of God does not say, "By the Law comes salvation." Salvation comes by faith in the grace of God: "The grace of God that bringeth salvation hath appeared to all men, teaching us that, denying ungodliness and worldly lusts, we should live soberly, righteously, and godly, in this present world" (Titus 2:11—12).

Verse 24: "Wherefore the Law was our schoolmaster to bring us unto Christ, that we might be justified by faith." Greek authorities tell us that the Greek for "schoolmaster" in the original——in the days when Christ walked upon the earth, and in the days when Paul ministered——was applied to a household servant who was put in charge of a child, to be a guide and tutor in that child's early years. When the child became of age the guide or tutor would turn him over to others. The Law was Israel's guide (or tutor) until Christ came, and shed His blood on the cross that they might be justified by faith in His shed blood. Every lamb that was slain and its blood offered during the Dispensation of Law, pointed to the shed blood of the Lamb of God on Calvary's cross; but the poor Jews were so spiritually blind they could not see their Lamb. All they could see was tradition and the religion of their fathers.

The Mosaic Covenant was given to Israel in three parts:

The first part: *The Commandments.* The Commandments expressed the righteous will of God concerning the nation Israel (Exodus 20:1–26).

The second part: *The Judgments,* governing the social life of Israel (Exodus 21:1 through Exodus 24:11).

The third part: *The Ordinances,* which governed the religious life of the Israelites (Exodus 24:12 through Exodus 31:18).

Verse 25: "BUT AFTER THAT FAITH IS COME, WE ARE NO LONGER UNDER A SCHOOLMASTER."

Could anything be clearer? The Law was our schoolmaster––up to Christ. But when the Lord Jesus came, we were no longer under a schoolmaster. We now have another teacher––the Holy Spirit. Jesus said, "I have yet many things to say unto you, but ye cannot bear them now. Howbeit when He, the Spirit of truth, is come, He will guide you into all truth: for He shall not speak of Himself; but whatsoever He shall hear, that shall He speak: and He will shew you things to come" (John 16:12–13). These words were spoken by Jesus to the disciples before His crucifixion and before Pentecost; but hear these words after the Holy Ghost was given:

"But ye have an unction from the Holy One, AND

YE KNOW ALL THINGS . . . but the anointing which ye have received (the Holy Ghost) of Him abideth in you, and ye need not that any man teach you: but as the same anointing teacheth you of all things, and is truth, and is no lie, and even as it hath taught you, ye shall abide in Him" (I John 2:20 and 27).

The apostles were not yet ready to receive the truth which the Holy Spirit would reveal to them after Pentecost. This special revelation was reserved by God to be given to the apostles (especially Paul) at the right time. Before Jesus came to this earth, revelation was given in type and shadow: "God, who at sundry times and in divers manners spake in time past unto the fathers by the prophets, hath in these last days spoken unto us by His Son . . ." (Heb. 1:1–2).

Verses 26–29: "For ye are all the children of God by faith in Christ Jesus. For as many of you as have been baptized into Christ have put on Christ. There is neither Jew nor Greek, there is neither bond nor free, there is neither male nor female: for ye are all one in Christ Jesus. And if ye be Christ's, then are ye Abraham's seed, and heirs according to the promise."

All believers, regardless of their color or nationality, are children of God. In verse 27 the baptism referred to is not water baptism. No one can be baptized by water into the body of Christ. I know you want proof for that statement so we will hear the testimony of the Scriptures:

"For as the body is one, and hath many members, and all the members of that one body, being many, are one body: so also is Christ. For by one Spirit are we all baptized into one body, whether we be Jews or Gentiles, whether we be bond or free; and have been all made to drink into one Spirit" (I Cor. 12:12–13).

From this Scripture we clearly see that all believers are baptized by the Spirit into the body of Christ. The baptizer is not the minister in the local church——but the risen Christ Himself. Read Matthew 3:11. He baptizes the believer in the Holy Spirit and into Himself, thereby making the believer a member of His (Christ's) own body . . . a member of His flesh and of His bones. Read Ephesians 5:30. This makes Christ and the born again believer *one flesh*. Study carefully Ephesians 5:29-31. It is imperative to understand this tremendous spiritual truth, if we would ever appreciate our position in Jesus by grace. Many dear believers are losing out in abundant living because of ignorance concerning our position in Christ as a child of God, a son of God, an heir of God and a joint-heir with Jesus Christ, even now sitting with Him in heavenly places (Eph. 2:6).

Paul goes on to point out that there is neither Jew nor Greek, neither bond nor free, neither male nor female . . . we are all one in Christ. All are baptized into one body by one Spirit. All are made to drink into one Spirit. The literal Greek reads, "YE ARE ALL ONE MAN IN CHRIST JESUS!" Then Paul points out that if we are Christ's, we are Abraham's seed, and heirs according to the promise. Since it is true that all believers are members of the body of Christ, and all believers constitute one man in Christ, then it is also true that those of us who are born again are the children of Abraham and will inherit the promise along with faithful Abraham. We are in Christ, we are members of His body. Therefore, the inheritance is not by Law, but by promise! The inheritance does not come through good works nor by keeping the Law; but only by Grace, through faith in the finished work of the Lord Jesus——plus nothing. It is Christ, all Christ, totally apart from man's work or man's ability. "Christ in you, the hope of glory . . . ye are complete in Him."

The saints in the Old Testament era could not see nor understand what we see and understand. The Old Testament saints since Moses were under the bondage of the Law. Thank God the New Testament saint (since Jesus came, paid sin's debt and became a curse for the sinner) is in the liberty that grace provides. During the Old Testament era, the believer, though an heir of God, was an infant (spiritually speaking). Today, when we embrace by faith the finished work of Jesus Christ and become a recipient of God's saving grace, we receive the position as adult sons. We will see this very clearly in chapter four.

GALATIANS — CHAPTER FOUR

1. Now I say, That the heir, as long as he is a child, differeth nothing from a servant, though he be lord of all;
2. But is under tutors and governors until the time appointed of the father.
3. Even so we, when we were children, were in bondage under the elements of the world:
4. But when the fulness of the time was come, God sent forth his Son, made of a woman, made under the law,
5. To redeem them that were under the law, that we might receive the adoption of sons.
6. And because ye are sons, God hath sent forth the Spirit of his Son into your hearts, crying, Abba, Father.
7. Wherefore thou art no more a servant, but a son; and if a son, then an heir of God through Christ.
8. Howbeit then, when ye knew not God, ye did service unto them which by nature are no gods.
9. But now, after that ye have known God, or rather are known of God, how turn ye again to the weak and beggarly elements, whereunto ye desire again to be in bondage?
10. Ye observe days, and months, and times, and years.
11. I am afraid of you, lest I have bestowed upon you labour in vain.
12. Brethren, I beseech you, be as I am; for I am as ye are: ye have not injured me at all.
13. Ye know how through infirmity of the flesh I preached the gospel unto you at the first.
14. And my temptation which was in my flesh ye despised not, nor rejected; but received me as an angel of God, even as Christ Jesus.
15. Where is then the blessedness ye spake of? for I bear you record, that, if it had been possible, ye would have plucked out your own eyes, and have given them to me.
16. Am I therefore become your enemy, because I tell you the truth?
17. They zealously affect you, but not well; yea, they would exclude you, that ye might affect them.
18. But it is good to be zealously affected always in a good thing, and not only when I am present with you.
19. My little children, of whom I travail in birth again until Christ be formed in you,
20. I desire to be present with you now, and to change my voice; for I stand in doubt of you.
21. Tell me, ye that desire to be under the law, do ye not hear the law?
22. For it is written, that Abraham had two sons, the one by a

bondmaid, the other by a freewoman.

23. But he who was of the bondwoman was born after the flesh; but he of the freewoman was by promise.

24. Which things are an allegory: for these are the two covenants; the one from the mount Sinai, which gendereth to bondage, which is Agar.

25. For this Agar is mount Sinai in Arabia, and answereth to Jerusalem which now is, and is in bondage with her children.

26. But Jerusalem which is above is free, which is the mother of us all.

27. For it is written, Rejoice, thou barren that bearest not; break forth and cry, thou that travailest not: for the desolate hath many more children than she which hath an husband.

28. Now we, brethren, as Isaac was, are the children of promise.

29. But as then he that was born after the flesh persecuted him that was born after the Spirit, even so it is now.

30. Nevertheless what saith the scripture? Cast out the bondwoman and her son: for the son of the bondwoman shall not be heir with the son of the freewoman.

31. So then, brethren, we are not children of the bondwoman, but of the free.

Verses 1–3: "Now I say, That the heir, as long as he is a child, differeth nothing from a servant, though he be lord of all; But is under tutors and governors until the time appointed of the father. Even so we (Jews—— Paul and his Jewish brethren) when we were children (that is, when the Dispensation of Law was running its course) WERE IN BONDAGE UNDER THE ELEMENTS OF THE WORLD."

Face it, beloved: The saint in the Old Testament era was a babe . . . immature, not realizing the glory and the fulness of his future inheritance in Christ. The Old Testament saint looked *forward* to the coming of the Lamb of God. We on this side of Calvary know that He HAS come and we have the precious written Word to prove it. We also have the testimony in our hearts, because the Holy Ghost abides in the bosom of every born again child of God (Romans 8:9).

The Old Testament saint was like a child who, though

heir to a large estate, is unable during his infancy to exercise his heirship or lordship. The Old Testament saint lived in shadows . . . he lived in the dimness of the Law. He was a child of God in his relationship, for he was born from above and born of God; but he did not yet have the relationship of sonship. He was in slavery under "the elements of the world," or the Law. *We* have the glorious light of Christ who said, "I am the Light of the world" (John 8:12). Today under Grace the shadows are gone, and we enjoy the revelation given to Paul and the other writers of the marvelous books of the New Testament.

THE DIFFERENCE? Verses 4 and 5 explain: "But when the fulness of the time was come, God sent forth His Son, made of a woman, made under the Law, to redeem them that were under the Law, that we might receive the adoption of sons."

The cross of the Lord Jesus stands between the Law of Moses and the Grace of God. BEFORE the cross of Jesus . . . before the shedding of the blood of the Lamb without spot or wrinkle or any such thing, there was no such thing as *putting away* sin. God pardoned the sinner, He suspended the judgment against the sinner, He covered the sin of the sinner; but this all pointed to the anticipated coming of THE REDEEMER, THE LORD JESUS CHRIST. Before Calvary, God pardoned the sinner and forgave his sin only upon the promise of the coming of the Lamb of God, the Lord Jesus Christ. Before the cross there was no FULL AND COMPLETE FORGIVENESS FOR THE SINNER; but AFTER the cross of Jesus, sin is put away; sin is blotted out in the blood, washed away in the blood . . . and our robes are made white in the blood (Rev. 1:5; Heb. 9:22; I John 1:7).

Before the Lord Jesus died, was buried, and rose

again "according to the Scriptures," all saints were placed in Sheol when they died. They remained there until Jesus was crucified and spent three days and three nights in the heart of the earth. On the third day He arose——and when He arose He led captivity captive . . . He brought the spirits of the saints out of Sheol and carried them to the Paradise far above all Heavens (Eph. 4:7–11). Please read Psalm 16:9–10. Since Calvary, the believer goes (at death) directly into the presence of God in Heaven . . . to be absent from the body is to be present with the Lord. The beggar Lazarus died and was carried by the angels into Abraham's bosom. To the thief on the cross, Jesus said, "Today shalt thou be with me in Paradise." The spirit of the believer does not go to Sheol in this day, but to be absent from the body is to be *instantaneously, immediately,* with the Lord Jesus.

In Genesis 3:15 God promised the seed of the woman. From that moment until the day Jesus was born, all hell did everything possible to prevent the seed that would bruise the serpent's head. Nevertheless, Jesus was born as prophesied. A virgin conceived (in spite of what Bishop Pike and others say) and brought forth a son, and called His name Jesus. The Holy Ghost overshadowed Mary and she brought forth a son named Emmanuel, interpreted "God with us."

The coming of Jesus was declared in Genesis 3:15. The promise was fulfilled on schedule . . . WHEN THE FULNESS OF TIME WAS COME. The birth of Jesus was also as prophesied——or promised——by Jehovah God in the Garden. GOD SENT FORTH HIS SON, MADE OF A WOMAN, MADE UNDER THE LAW. God was the Father of Jesus. No man had any part in His birth. The virgin Mary conceived when she was overshadowed by the Holy Ghost (Luke 1; Matthew 1). God always does exactly what He promises, exactly as He promised. So—— When the fulness of time was come, God sent forth His only begotten Son, made of a woman, made under the Law, sent to redeem them that were under the Law, that we "might receive the adoption of sons." (The "we" in this verse refers to the Jew, because it was the Jew who was under the Law of Moses. The Law was never given to Gentiles, but only to Israel.) Jesus came to redeem those who were under the Law, that these people who were in bondage might receive the adoption of sons. In this glorious Dispensation of the marvelous Grace of God, Jews, Gentiles, rich, poor, bond, free, learned or unlearned become sons of God when they put their faith and trust in the finished work of the Lord Jesus Christ.

Verse 6: "And because ye are sons, God hath sent forth the Spirit of His Son into your hearts, crying, Abba, Father."

There are those who teach that it is possible to be saved and yet not possess the Holy Ghost; but such teaching is false and foreign to the Word of God. It is the Holy Ghost who indwells us. Please read I Corinthians 6:19—20. It is the Holy Spirit who enables us to realize our position in Christ . . . sons, heirs of God, and joint-heirs with Christ. It is the Holy Spirit who brings us into such a place of intimacy and closeness with God that we cry unto Him, "Abba, Father!" The word "Abba" comes to us from Hebrew, untranslated. Hebrew authorities tell us that the pure translation of the word means "Papa." I do not know whether or not you called your dad "Papa," but I was reared in an old-fashioned home and we children (nine of us) always referred to our parents as "mama" and "papa." I never called my daddy by the name of "father" or "daddy." I always referred to him as "papa."

Just as the first word a baby learns is either "papa"

or "mama," the Holy Spirit would have us also to call upon God in the Spirit of sonship, crying, "Papa, Father." The word "papa" is an endearing term, it is tender . . . and the Lord Jesus Himself used the same expression in Gethsemane when He prayed to the Heavenly Father: "Abba, Father, all things are possible unto thee; take away this cup from me: nevertheless not what I will, but what thou wilt" (Mark 14:36).

The same Holy Ghost who abides in our bosom certainly directed the prayer of the Man Christ Jesus as He prayed in the Garden of Gethsemane, helping Him to trust Himself unreservedly and wholeheartedly to the Heavenly Father . . . "Papa, Father"; and to totally depend upon and trust in God's will and God's judgment. The Holy Ghost would have us place our total dependence upon the Heavenly Father, and would lead us tenderly to trust God with all of our heart, to call upon the Heavenly Father as a son would speak to his papa. God wants us to think of Him as a Father, a papa, who is concerned about each and every minute detail of our living. Read Romans 8:15.

Verse 7: "Wherefore thou art no more a servant, BUT A SON; and if a son, then an heir of God through Christ."

Those who are under Law are servants; but thank God, those who are under Grace are sons—born sons of God through the finished work of the Lord Jesus Christ. Anyone knows that a servant works for wages. A son works because of love and personal interest in the papa of the family. There is a gigantic difference between working for a *boss* and working for papa. Under the boss we certainly work with a different spirit; we have a different attitude toward him as compared with our own dear parent. Under the Law (as a boss) the service was *commanded*—and of course the threat of penalty went along with the command. Under Grace it is our love for our Father that causes us to do what we do joyfully and gladly . . . even to the giving of our money. "God loveth a cheerful giver," and whatever we do we should do diligently from a heart full of cheerfulness for the very privilege of doing what we do to the glory of God.

A servant could never call his master "papa" . . . that endearing term is reserved for the children; but Paul uses the expression when referring to sons of God praying to the Heavenly Father as sons . . . "For ye have not received the spirit of bondage again to fear (THAT IS, THE FEAR OF THE LAW OF MOSES); but ye have received the Spirit of adoption, whereby we cry, Abba, Father" (Rom. 8:15).

In Romans 8:16 Paul reveals a tremendous truth: "The Spirit (Himself) beareth witness with our spirit, that we are the children of God." The word "Abba" is used only by the children of God who are saved by grace through faith plus nothing . . . and who live under Grace.

Verses 8 and 9: "Howbeit then, when ye knew not God, ye did service unto them which by nature are no gods. But now, after that ye have known God, or rather are known of God, how turn ye again to the weak and beggarly elements, whereunto ye desire again to be in bondage?"

Note in the first part of verse 8 the word "YE." Paul does not mean the Jews. It is plain that he means the Gentiles. Had he meant the Jews he would have said, "WE." The Jews had head-knowledge of God under the Law, but Paul says, "When YE knew not God," and certainly he was speaking of the Gentiles. It amazed Paul that these Gentiles would turn again to the beggarly elements after having experienced the marvelous liberty of the Grace of God (and the peace that Grace brings to the individual heart) after they had been set free from bondage. Paul could not understand their desire to return to the bondage of the Law.

I imagine these Gentile believers at Galatia were a bit shocked when Paul made the statement that they were turning again to idolatry. I am sure they must have asked among themselves, "How could returning to the Law be idolatry?" They probably made it clear to Paul that they were only taking up the *principle* of the Law——and surely he would not call this "weak and beggarly elements." Paul reminded them that before they were converted, they worshipped false gods and idols. He stated to the believers in Thessalonica, "For they themselves shew of us what manner of entering in we had unto you, and how ye turned to God from idols to serve the living and true God; and to wait for His Son from heaven, whom He raised from the dead, even Jesus, which delivered us from the wrath to come" (I Thess. 1:9—10).

Paul goes on to warn, "If you Christians go back to Jewish principles, feast days, and the rituals of Judaism, you are certainly, in principle, idolators again! Why would you turn back to idolatry from which God has delivered you? How could you do this?" Do not entertain the idea that Paul was saying that the Law was unholy or idolatrous . . . not so at all; but he makes it very clear to the believers, writing in the book of Hebrews: "For if we sin wilfully after that we have received the knowledge of the truth, there remaineth no more sacrifice for sins" (Heb. 10:26). Just what does that verse mean . . . "If we go on sinning wilfully after we have received the knowledge of the truth"? Jesus said, "I am the truth." Again He said, "Sanctify them through thy truth: thy Word is truth" (John 14:6; John 17:17).

Jesus is truth, the Word is truth, Jesus and the Word are one. "In the beginning was the Word, the Word was with God, and the Word was God . . . and the Word became flesh . . . ." The truth is the Word. After we have received the good news of the Gospel, "there remaineth no more sacrifice for sin." In other words, Jesus offered His blood "once, for all, forever." No other sacrifice can be made . . . He made the supreme sacrifice . . . He satisfied the heart of God, the holiness of God, the commandments of God; therefore, "there remaineth no more sacrifice." After the Galatians had heard about the shed blood of Jesus, the good news of the Gospel, if they turned from that Gospel back to Judaism they were idolators.

You need not go to Africa, China, Japan, India . . . or to the jungles of Brazil to find idol-worshippers. America is full of them! Thousands of them belong to fashionable denominational churches. There are thousands of church members who worship the building . . . some even worship the steeple. Some worship the pipe organ; some worship the rugs on the floor; some worship the pews. Anything that is foremost in your mind, anything that you spend the most time thinking about and loving, is your idol, regardless of what it is. So——if the Galatians returned to the rituals of Judaism, they were idolators.

Today, when professing Christians take up the Law, with its external ceremonies and shadows, when they adopt the practice of the Law in supposed-to-be Christian worship, it is idolatry.

We are saved by God's grace, through faith. We are kept by the power of God. "The just shall live by faith" . . . and "whatsoever is not of faith is sin." This business of placing articles in the church or in the home to help in worship, is idolatry, regardless of what you think of it or what your preacher has to say about it. Such practice is not only in the Catholic church, but it is being taken up by thousands of Protestant churches. Any trinket, any image, anything——regardless of what it is——if it has any religious element at all, it is idolatrous. Supposing a person were to say, "I find myself very cold in worshipping God, and I want something to arouse my soul; what more proper thing could I have than a picture of my Saviour, that as I look upon Him and upon His crown of thorns, I may feel more deeply His love and have my heart's affections more drawn out to Him?" That is idolatry. To make use of anything in worship to increase feelings or religious awe, or to see with the eye or to hear with the ear, to assist in worship using the fallen nature to produce religious feelings or to help in religious worship is certainly idolatry. Certainly it is opposed to naked faith. Faith accepts God because He is God. Faith accepts Jesus because of what God tells us about Him in the Bible. Faith believes without seeing, feeling, tasting, or smelling. Faith does not ask for proof. Faith accepts without proof. The Bible begins thus:

"IN THE BEGINNING GOD . . ." (Gen. 1:1). I have written in the margin of my first Bible, these words: "I believe all the rest!" Why not write something like that in *your* Bible? If God *said* it, you can *believe* it. You may not understand it . . . you may never understand it . . . but the just shall live by faith——not by wisdom nor by understanding. The just shall live by faith . . . not by proof nor by feelings. *The just shall live by faith!* We do not need any little trinkets in the home, on the dashboard in our automobile, around our neck or in our purse or billfold. All we need is the Holy Ghost in our heart by faith——and if He abides in our bosom we are more than conquerors through the Lord Jesus who loved us, because we are kept by the power of God; and "this is the victory that overcometh the world, EVEN OUR FAITH!"

It is an insult to Almighty God to use the weak and beggarly elements to assist in worshipping a Holy God who is an eternal Spirit and who must be worshipped in spirit and in truth.

Verse 10: "Ye observe days, and months, and times, and years."

The Galatians were swiftly returning to formal religious systems; and cold, formal religious systems can produce only dead services and superficial worship. God hates such "carryings on"; God longs for true worship from the heart. It is a sad thing when a church has a name of being alive because of the beautiful edifice, the great crowds, the robed choir, the pipe organ and the chimes in the steeple! But John tells us in Revelation 3:1 that a certain group had a name that they were alive ——although they were dead. I am sure we have many of those groups with us today——sad but so. Beautiful buildings, beautiful services, an educated minister with all of his religious garb and program; all of the risings and sittings, all of the beautiful sayings and the "singing in" and "singing out" of the services is not necessarily pleasing to Almighty God. He wants to be worshipped in spirit and in truth.

THE DEPARTED BLESSING

Verse 11: "I am afraid of you, lest I have bestowed upon you labour in vain." Paul was beginning to fear that his work was coming to nought, that he had labored and sacrificed in vain in the ministry he had bestowed upon the Galatians. Paul was a dedicated minister. He had a deep feeling for his converts in the grace of God.

He felt the same about all of the churches the Holy Ghost had used him to establish. "As ye know how we exhorted and comforted and charged every one of you, AS A FATHER DOTH HIS CHILDREN" (I Thess. 2:11). Paul felt toward his converts as a true father feels toward his sons. The fear he mentions here was not for himself, but for the believers at Galatia. His heart yearned over them, and burned for them as the heart of a loving father for his children.

Verse 12: "Brethren, I beseech you, be as I am; for I am as ye are: ye have not injured me at all." What Paul is literally saying here is: "I beseech you, brethren, *become as I am*, for I also am become as ye are." Paul had forsaken his high position as a Jew. He was born into a very elite family . . . it had cost him a great deal to forsake his position as a Jew under the Law. He had taken his place with the Gentile believers at Galatia as sinners—hopeless, helpless, hell-bound. He had taken his place along with them depending wholly and entirely upon the Grace of God for salvation . . . Grace plus nothing. But now the Galatian believers were forsaking their position under Grace, and turning to Paul's former position under the Law. In the eyes of Paul, they were so foolish! He assures them it is not sympathy he is seeking, for he says, "Ye have not injured me at all."

Verses 13 and 14: "Ye know how through infirmity of the flesh I preached the Gospel unto you at the first. And my temptation which was in my flesh ye despised not, nor rejected; but received me as an angel of God, even as Christ Jesus."

Undoubtedly Paul was referring to the injuries resulting from the horrible stoning he had undergone at Lystra, when he was dragged outside the city for dead (Acts 14:19—20; II Cor. 12:1—10). He must have been injured severely, probably marred and scarred as a result of that terrible ordeal. Because of that horrible flogging, he did not make his intended missionary journeys, but turned to the Galatians and preached the Gospel to them. The Galatians had much to be thankful for. It was because of Paul's infirmity of the flesh that they heard the Gospel for the first time. Paul now reminds them that when he came to them the first time in weakness, preaching the pure Grace of God, they did not turn him away because of his infirmities. They did not despise nor reject him because of his injury; but they had received him as God's messenger. They received him even as they would have received Jesus Christ . . . they did everything but make a god of him! (He would not have permitted them to carry it that far, had they attempted it.)

Verse 15: "Where is then the blessedness ye spake of? for I bear you record, that if it had been possible, ye would have plucked out your own eyes, and have given them to me."

I have already pointed out that Paul was brutally beaten, stoned and dragged outside the city of Lystra for dead. It would seem that he was injured severely about the eyes, which injury not only interfered with his vision but also caused his facial appearance to be far from attractive. Greek authorities tell us that the Greek word for "rejected" in verse 14, literally rendered, would have been "spat out." This indicates that Paul's appearance was certainly repulsive, and those who looked upon him could have been tempted to turn away. They could have refused to hear the message of a man so marred and scarred in his appearance. Please read Isaiah 52: 13–14, also Isaiah 53:2–4.

The Bible clearly states that Paul had a "thorn in the flesh." Many outstanding Bible authorities believe this thorn was his eyesight, that he was almost blind; and it could be that this impaired vision was the result of the terrible stoning at Lystra.

Verse 16: "Am I therefore become your enemy, because I tell you the truth?" Every true Bible witness of God knows how easy it is for those who profess to be best friends to very quickly turn and become a bitter enemy, doing exactly the opposite of what they had been accustomed to do. Love and respect can turn to hatred and contempt. Once the Galatians would have plucked out their eyes and have given them to Paul——but now they seem to be becoming his enemies because he refused to compromise with their legalism . . . because he dogmatically and without apology preached *salvation by Grace through faith*——plus nothing.

To the Corinthian believers Paul said, "Have I committed an offence in abasing myself that ye might be exalted, because I have preached to you the gospel of God freely? . . . Wherefore? because I love you not? God knoweth" (II Cor. 11:7–11). Paul had a heavy heart when he uttered the words in Galatians 4:16. I can almost hear the quivering of his voice as he tenderly looked upon the people who had so willingly accepted the message of Grace, who were so happy in the *liberty* of Grace. As he looked upon them . . . victims of the legalizers . . . he said, "Am I therefore become your enemy? The man for whom you would have plucked out your own eyes, the one whom you would have set up as Jesus Christ? Am I now your enemy because I refuse to lie to you? Because I refuse to compromise and preach a half-truth? Am I your enemy because I preach the truth without fear, favor or apology?" You may rest assured that the Apostle Paul would never have deviated from the message of the cross to keep the friendship of any person, regardless of who that person might be. If he were alive today he would be the same Paul——because he was called of God, ordained of God, commissioned of God, sent by God . . . therefore he preached the Gospel. All of *God's* preachers preach the Gospel. Hirelings preach to please people; God's ministers preach to please God Almighty.

Verses 17 and 18: "They zealously affect you, but not well; yea, they would exclude you, that ye might affect them. But it is good to be zealously affected always in a good thing, and not only when I am present with you."

Literally Paul is saying, "They zealously seek you in no good way; nay, they desire to shut you out, that ye may seek them. But it is good to be zealously sought in a good manner at all times AND NOT ONLY WHEN I AM PRESENT WITH YOU."

Writing to the believers at Corinth, Paul said practically the same thing to them: "But what I do, that I will do, that I may cut off occasion from them which desire occasion; that wherein they glory, they may be found even as we. For such are false apostles, deceitful workers, transforming themselves into the apostles of Christ. And no marvel; for Satan himself is transformed into an angel of light. Therefore it is no great thing if his ministers also be transformed as the ministers of righteousness; whose end shall be according to their works" (II Cor. 11:12–15).

I often make the statement in my meetings that not everyone who stands behind the sacred desk is God's preacher. Not everyone who has a degree from a seminary is God's preacher. Not everyone who wears a scissortail coat, with his collar turned backward, is God's man. The devil has ordained ministers just as surely as God has ordained ministers. You may rest assured that all who claim to be ministers of the Gospel are NOT ministers of the Gospel. Satan himself is transformed as an angel of light, and therefore it is certainly not astonishing that his ministers be transformed (or appear) as ministers of righteousness . . . "but their end shall be according to their works." The devil has a cheap counterfeit for everything good that God has provided in Jesus Christ through Grace. Beware of the minister who mixes Law and Grace——or who mixes *anything* with Grace. God's preachers preach salvation by Grace, through faith, plus nothing.

LAW AND GRACE CANNOT COEXIST

Verses 19 and 20: "My little children, of whom I travail in birth again until Christ be formed in you, I desire to be present with you now, and to change my voice; for I stand in doubt of you." Face it, beloved: What Paul is really saying here is, "I am afraid you Galatians are not fully born." Paul feared that they had not fully and wholeheartedly accepted the Grace of God.

It is altogether possible for a person to go a long way, to demonstrate what seems to be real Christianity, and yet not be truly born again. You cannot look at people and declare that they are truly born again. You cannot listen to their testimony and vow that they are saved. The devil is shrewd——and if he can cause a sinner to stop short of salvation by Grace through faith plus nothing, he is extremely happy. The devil can send a person to hell much more easily *in* religion than *out of* religion. A person who is religious (but lost) is much more difficult to reach with the Gospel of Grace than is a person who has never known anything about salvation by Grace through faith. Please study carefully I Thessalonians 2:7—11. Notice the message to the believers at Thessalonica.

It was difficult for Paul (in writing) to make these

Galatians realize just how deeply concerned he was for them, and how much he wished he might be present with them instead of writing. He was perplexed about them, and very deeply concerned over them.

Verse 21: "Tell me, ye that desire to be under the Law, do ye not hear the Law?" Here is another of Paul's questions. He is reminding the Galatians that when the Law was given at Sinai the people were removed a great distance from God. When the Law was given on Sinai, there were thunders and lightnings and a thick cloud upon the mountain; and the voice of the trumpet was exceeding loud, so that all the people who were in the camp trembled. Mount Sinai was altogether on a smoke, because Jehovah descended upon it in fire, and the smoke thereof ascended as the smoke of a furnace. The whole mountain quaked. Read Exodus 19:16–18. All the people of Israel witnessed the thunderings and lightnings, and heard the noise of the trumpet; they saw the mountain smoking, and when they saw it they removed and stood afar off. They said to Moses, "Speak thou with us and we will hear: but let not God speak with us, LEST WE DIE!" Read Exodus 20:18–19.

To the Galatians Paul is saying, "Is this what you want? Is this what you are returning to? After having tasted the Grace of God, after having enjoyed the liberty of God's marvelous Grace, do you desire to return to the thundering, the lightning, the clouds, the quaking of the mountain . . . the smoke? Is that what you want?" Hallelujah! How wonderful it is to know that believers today are not under the Law!

"And it came to pass on the third day in the morning, that there were thunders and lightnings, and a thick cloud upon the mount, and the voice of the trumpet exceeding loud; so that all the people that was in the camp trembled. And Moses brought forth the people out of the camp to meet with God; and they stood at the nether part of the mount. And mount Sinai was altogether on a smoke, because the Lord descended upon it in fire: and the smoke thereof ascended as the smoke of a furnace, and the whole mount quaked greatly" (Exodus 19:16—18). Hallelujah for Grace! Thank God, "Christ is the end of the Law for righteousness to everyone that believeth" (Rom. 10:4).

In Galatians the question Paul is answering is not the question of Law AND Grace——but it is the solemn, eternal question of whether it is Law OR Grace. It cannot be Law AND Grace——because Grace and Law do not mix. It is either one or the other. For a person to testify that he is saved by Grace, but must keep himself by *works*, is to deny Grace. The Grace of God that brings salvation teaches us to deny ungodliness and worldly lusts, and to live soberly, righteously and godly in this present world (Titus 2:11—15). When God saves the sinner, He puts the Holy Ghost into the bosom of that sinner, and sets up a classroom in the heart, with the Grace of God as the professor . . . *the Grace of God teaches us.* God's Grace does not save us and then leave us to fight our own battles. The Grace of God abides within.

As an illustration, Paul uses the account of Abraham and his two sons:

Verses 22—26: "For it is written, that Abraham had two sons, the one by a bondmaid, the other by a freewoman. But he who was of the bondwoman was born after the flesh; but he of the freewoman was by promise. Which things are an allegory: for these are the two covenants; the one from the mount Sinai, which gendereth to bondage, which is Agar. For this Agar is mount Sinai in Arabia, and answereth to Jerusalem which now is, and is in bondage with her children. But Jerusalem which is above is free, which is the mother of us all."

Paul had a burning desire to set straight these Galatian believers who had been confused by the legalizers. He went back into Bible history and used Abraham as an illustration. He reminded the Galatians that Abraham had two wives——a bondmaiden, and his true wife, Sarah. He contrasts Hagar (the Egyptian slave girl) with Sarah, the wife of promise, the wife God gave to Abraham. Paul likens Hagar to the Law, and compares Sarah to the Grace of God. Then he mentions the two sons . . . Ishmael, the son of the bondwoman (born after the flesh, by the will of man), and Isaac, the miracle-child, supernaturally born by promise——the promise of Almighty God who cannot lie.

God had nothing to do with the birth of Ishmael. You know the story as told in Genesis. Sarah reminded Abraham that surely God had forgotten His promise that a son would be born to them. Therefore Sarah suggested to Abraham that he go in to Hagar and perchance *she* could give to him a son. Instead of listening to God Almighty, Abraham (like Adam) listened to his wife and did as she suggested. As a result, Ishmael was born after the flesh, while Isaac was the child of promise.

Paul then said, "These two women, Hagar and Sarah, and their two sons, Ishmael and Isaac, are an allegory. They have a spiritual application, and this story is given for our instruction." It was Paul who said, "ALL Scripture is given by inspiration of God, and is profitable for doctrine, for reproof, for correction, for instruction in righteousness" (II Tim. 3:16). The two women and their sons are symbolic of Law and Grace. Paul uses the allegory to illustrate his message of salvation by Grace through faith plus nothing.

The story of Hagar and Sarah, with their two sons, was not put in the Bible to fill up space. It was recorded to teach a spiritual lesson. The Scriptures clearly point out that Ishmael was born of the will of the flesh, and the fact of his birth reveals Abraham's terrible failure and weakness *in* the flesh. It was in the flesh that Abraham attempted to help God fulfill His promise. *Because* Abraham was flesh, he had given up hope concerning God's promise that a child would be born, through which the Seed would come. Abraham, because of the flesh, could not fully believe God concerning this promise, seeing that he and Sarah were getting old and still God had given them no son. But God had made a promise to Abraham——and He was able to keep that promise. Abraham decided he would help God by going in unto Hagar the bondwoman——a symbol of bondage, a symbol of doubt and failure . . . failure to trust God. Paul uses Abraham's failure, and illustrates man's attempt to please God by the works of the flesh. Hagar represents the Law. Ishmael represents the works of the flesh, which of course always bring about bondage. Paul goes further to point out that in addition to Sarah and Hagar and their two sons, Ishmael and Isaac, there are two covenants also involved: The Covenant of the Law of Mount Sinai, and the Covenant of Grace which had its beginning at Mount Calvary when Jesus was crucified. Then he speaks of two cities——the Jerusalem of Paul's day, and the New Jerusalem . . . the eternal abode of the redeemed, the bride of Christ, the New Testament church. Thus, in Paul's illustration we have two women (Hagar and Sarah); two sons (Ishmael and Isaac); two covenants (Law and Grace); two mountains (Sinai and Calvary); two cities (the earthly Jerusalem and the Pearly White City, the New Jerusalem which John saw descending from God out of Heaven). Paul points out all of this in detail, to show the difference between salvation by Grace through faith plus nothing, and the attempt to be saved by Grace plus Law-works. Hagar, Ishmael, Mount Sinai and the earthly Jerusalem are all pictures of the Law. Hagar was a slave, and in the spiritual sense the Law makes slaves of those who are under the Law. What astonished Paul was how anyone could return to the Law, knowing that the Law brought bondage while Grace brought liberty. ". . . FROM THE MOUNT SINAI, WHICH GENDERETH TO BONDAGE" (Gal. 4:24).

But Paul does not stop here. He continues by saying that the Law which was given to Moses on Mount Sinai could not set anyone free . . . never did set anyone free . . . nor could it ever set anyone free. The Law of Sinai brings only bondage (Gal. 4:24). Perhaps Paul looked toward Jerusalem and asked the Galatians, "What is the condition of the City of Jerusalem? Look at that city! She was once a proud city, the capital of Palestine, the seat of the mighty King David . . . the envy of the world in the days of Solomon. Look at Jerusalem now!" In Paul's day Jerusalem was overrun by the foreign Gentile power of Rome——stripped of her freedom, the seat of a pagan Roman governor! And why? Simply because Israel tried to be kept by the Law . . . and failed. They broke every law God ever gave them. ". . . This Agar is Mount Sinai . . . and answereth to Jerusalem which now is, and is in bondage with her children" (Gal. 4:25). Hagar, being a slave, could bear only slave children. The Law of Moses could not make Hagar free, the Law of Moses could not make Ishmael free, nor make him the heir of promise. Mount Sinai did not send forth a message that brought hope to Israel——Sinai produces only slavery. God's Covenant of Works offered no eternal salvation and liberty to Israel as a nation; but only judgment, bondage, condemnation. Therefore Paul thunders out: "TELL ME, YE THAT DESIRE TO BE UNDER

THE LAW, WILL YOU STOP FOR A MOMENT AND LET ME TELL YOU WHAT THE LAW REALLY IS AND WHAT THE LAW REALLY DOES?"

After Paul had shown that the Law could not bring liberty, but could bring only bondage, he then cried out, "BUT JERUSALEM WHICH IS ABOVE IS FREE, WHICH IS THE MOTHER OF US ALL!" (Gal. 4:26). The Law could bring only fear; the Grace of God brings peace and assurance, and joy unspeakable and full of glory. Writing to the Hebrew believers, Paul said, "For ye are not come unto the mount that might be touched, and that burned with fire, nor unto blackness, and darkness, and tempest, and the sound of a trumpet, and the voice of words; which voice they that heard intreated that the word should not be spoken to them any more: (For they could not endure that which was commanded, And if so much as a beast touch the mountain, it shall be stoned, or thrust through with a dart: And so terrible was the sight, that Moses said, I exceedingly fear and quake:) But ye are come unto mount Sion, and unto the city of the living God, the heavenly Jerusalem, and to an innumerable company of angels, to the general assembly and church of the firstborn, which are written in heaven, and to God the Judge of all, and to the spirits of just men made perfect, and to Jesus the mediator of the new covenant, and to the blood of sprinkling, that speaketh better things than that of Abel" (Heb. 12:18—24).

Paul closes the allegory by saying:

Verses 27—31: "For it is written, Rejoice, thou barren that bearest not; break forth and cry, thou that travailest not: for the desolate hath many more children than she which hath an husband. Now we, brethren, as Isaac was, are the children of promise. But as then he that was born after the flesh persecuted him that was born after the Spirit, even so it is now. Nevertheless what saith the Scripture? Cast out the bondwoman and her son: for the son of the bondwoman shall not be heir with the son of the freewoman. So then, brethren, we are not children of the bondwoman, but of the free."

May I remind you that Ishmael, the son of Hagar, was the first-born in Abraham's tent. The Law was given first. Grace and truth were revealed later, in Jesus Christ. "For the Law was given by Moses, but grace and truth came by Jesus Christ" (John 1:17). The firstborn of Abraham (Ishmael) was set aside. The promised son (Isaac), sent by God through miraculous power, was the heir of promise. So the Law, which came first, could not save, and it was imperative that it be abandoned as a means of salvation, justification, and redemption. We must be saved by Grace, and Grace alone; therefore, the first becomes the last and the last becomes the first. The barren wife, Sarah (given to Abraham by God), becoming fruitful, set aside the bondwoman, the woman of the flesh. Grace supercedes the Law. Therefore, Paul closes this part of his message (an argument for salvation by Grace through faith plus nothing) by saying, "We brethren, as Isaac was, are the children of promise. We are not children because of the Law; we are children because of the promise." He then goes on to point out, "It is now as it was then . . . He that was born after the flesh persecuted him that was born after the Spirit. Nevertheless, what does the Scripture say? The Scriptures say, CAST OUT THE BONDWOMAN AND HER SON, FOR THE SON OF THE BONDWOMAN SHALL NOT BE HEIR WITH THE SON OF THE FREEWOMAN!"

Do you not see, beloved . . . Law and Grace cannot coexist, they cannot co-heir. It must be one or the other ——and the Scriptures say, "Cast out the bondwoman!

Cast out Hagar! Cast out Ishmael! He cannot be heir with the son of the freewoman. SO THEN BRETHREN, WE ARE NOT CHILDREN OF THE BONDWOMAN, BUT OF THE FREE!" We are not sons of God because of the Law. We are sons of God by Grace through faith plus nothing!

Let me remind you, dearly beloved, that according to God's holy Word, things are today as they were when Paul uttered these solemn words. The great-great-great-grandchildren of the legalizers and Judaizers of Paul's day are still with us. They are still persecuting the preachers of pure Grace, they oppose the message of salvation by Grace through faith plus nothing. They always add their little "do's and don'ts." They must put their hands upon you, they must baptize you according to their formula and you must sign their rules of doctrine or you shall surely roast in hell! They scream long and loud, "Grace! Grace! God's Grace! Grace that will pardon and cleanse within. Grace! Grace! God's Grace! Grace that is greater than all our sin." Then when they finish screaming "Grace!" they invite you to sign on the dotted line, to promise to be faithful to a program, a denomination . . . and to be sure to "bring all the tithes into the storehouse" and occupy eighteen inches of the same church pew every time the door opens, regardless of when, for what, or who will be speaking!

Dear reader, it might do you good to stop dead still and ask yourself the question, "Am I supporting a minister who preaches Grace? or a legalizer who makes laws and commands his parishioners to obey them?" No, no! Things have not changed one iota since the days of Paul. The most vicious opposition I ever have from any group is because of my message of salvation by Grace, through faith, plus nothing! There is not one single, solitary thing any man can do to help God save him, or to make himself better saved. Salvation is the Lord . . . "Christ in you, the hope of glory." "There is therefore now no condemnation to them which are in Christ Jesus!"

I do wish some precious ministers would preach some Sunday morning on these words: "Let no man therefore judge you in meat, or in drink, or in respect of an holyday, or of the new moon, or of the Sabbath days: WHICH ARE A SHADOW OF THINGS TO COME; but the body is of Christ" (Col. 2:16—17). The fact that the Law does not and cannot justify a sinner is certainly not a sign that the Law is a failure, or that the Law is weak. The Law is holy . . . but it cannot save a sinner. It was not *given* to save a sinner. God gave the Law to prove to man that man could not be saved by Law-works . . . rituals, the keeping of days, assemblies, Sabbaths, etc. The Law was given to point out the exceeding sinfulness of sin and the total depravity of man. The Law is perfect, the Law is holy. Man is imperfect, man is unholy. Therefore the natural man cannot keep the Law of God. The Law is just, man is unjust. The Law cannot show mercy to a guilty, condemned criminal. "All have sinned and come short of the glory of God . . . There is not a just man upon the earth that doeth good and sinneth not . . . There is none righteous, no, not one." Therefore we are all guilty before God; the Law can only testify against us and cry out, "The wages of sin is death!" "Cursed is everyone that continueth not in all things that are written in the book of the Law, to do them!" (Gal. 3:10). Therefore, any person who breaks the least of the commandments must be condemned by the commandment he has broken. Since we have all broken God's Law, the Law *condemns* all. All we like sheep have gone astray——but hallelujah! God has laid upon Jesus the iniquity of us all! So . . . in Christ, by

Grace, through faith, we become sons of God. Thank God for Calvary, where our sins were dealt with by the sin-less, virgin-born Son of God!

"Believe on the Lord Jesus Christ, and thou shalt be saved!" Salvation is a gift. The only way to obtain a gift and make it your own is to receive it (with thanksgiving) from the giver. God so loved sinners, He gave His only begotten Son to die on the cruel cross and take our place on Calvary, that we by receiving Him would be born into God's family by the power of God. We who receive Jesus are sons of God (John 1:12–13).

I have found the following study very interesting and helpful. Please read all of these verses and study them carefully. They have to do with Law and Grace:

1. Under Law there was a dividing veil (Ex. 26:33). Grace brought a rent veil (Heb. 10:19–22).

2. Law blots out the sinner (Ex. 32:33). Grace blots out the sinner's sin (Col. 2:14).

3. The Law curses the offender (Gal. 3:10). Grace covers the offender (Rom. 4:7).

4. The Law cries out, "*Do*—and live!" (Deut. 8:1). Grace cries out, "It is done! It is finished! Receive Jesus and live!" (John 19:30; John 1:12).

5. The Law cries out, "Every mouth stopped" (Rom. 3:19).
Grace invites, "Every mouth opened . . . that if thou shalt confess with thy mouth the Lord Jesus" (Rom. 10:9). "Whosoever shall call upon the name of the Lord" (Rom. 10:13).

6. The Law showed favor to the good (Prov. 12:2). The Grace of God shows mercy and favor to the bad, the ungodly (Eph. 2:1–6).

7. The Law was graven upon stone . . . outward (II Cor. 3:3).
   Grace is graven on the heart . . . inward . . . Christ in you (Col. 1:27; Col. 3:3; II Cor. 3:3).

8. The Law says, "He added no more" (Deut. 5:22).
   Grace assures us, "Hath spoken by His Son" (Heb. 1:2).

9. Law is inexorable in its demand (Josh. 7:25).
   The Grace of God is inspirational in its blessing (II Cor. 5:17).

10. The Law brings judgment (Rom. 5:18).
    Grace brings justification (Rom. 3:24).

11. Law cries out, "Keep the Commandments—all of them, in every minute detail" (James 2:10).
    Grace assures us we are kept by the power of God (I Peter 1:5).

12. The Law demands love (Deut. 6:5).
    The Grace of God exhibits love (John 3:16).

13. The Law moves the sinner to sin (Rom. 7:8).
    The Grace of God removes sin from the sinner (Matt. 1:21).

14. According to the Law, nearness to God is impossible (Ex. 20:21).
    In Grace, nearness to God is guaranteed (Eph. 2:13).

15. The Law demands obedience——or no blessing (Deut. 28:1–2).
    Grace brings obedience *because* of the blessing (I John 4:19).

16. The Law cries out, "Stone the prodigal" (Deut. 21:20–21).

Grace cries out, "Put the best robe on the prodigal . . . kill the fatted calf! Let us feast and be merry!" (Luke 15:20—22).

17. Law brings death (Deut. 21:22—23).
    Grace gives to us the quietness and assurance of peace (Rom. 5:1).

18. The Law retaliates (Ex. 21:24).
    The Grace of God redeems (Gal. 3:13).

19. The Law *demands* sanctification (Lev. 11:44).
    Grace *bestows* sanctification (I Cor. 1:30).

20. Because of the Law, three thousand were slain (Ex. 32:28).
    Because of the Grace of God, three thousand were saved (Acts 2:41).

21. The Law is unsatisfying to the conscience (Heb. 10:1—2).
    The Grace of God is unfailing in its forgiveness and remedy for sin (Heb. 9:12—14; Heb. 10:10—14).

22. The Law is the voice of consternation (Heb. 12:18—21).
    The Grace of God is the voice of covenant, blessing, peace and assurance (Heb. 12:22—24).

23. When the Law was given, Moses' face shown, and the people feared (Ex. 34:30).
    Grace brought by Jesus Christ attracted the people to the face of Jesus (Mark 9:15).

24. The Law was a yoke of burdensome weight (Gal. 5:1).
    Grace is to be in the yoke with Jesus, which makes the yoke easy and the burden light (Matt. 11:29—30).

25. The Law produced zeal (Rom. 10:1—2), but no

salvation (Phil. 3:6; Rom. 10:1–8).

Grace imparts zeal, and brings joy unspeakable and full of glory because we are saved (Titus 2:14; I Pet. 1:8).

I am so thankful that "Christ is the end of the Law for righteousness to everyone that believeth!" These facts are precious to me:

We are "accepted in the Beloved" (Eph. 1:6).

We are "blessed with all spiritual blessings" (Eph. 1:3).

We are called the sons of God (I John 3:1).

We are delivered from the wrath to come (I Thess. 1:10).

We are the elect of God (I Thess. 1:4).

We are forgiven by God (Eph. 1:7) for Christ's sake (Eph. 4:32).

We are saved by the grace of God (Eph. 2:5).

We are an holy priesthood (I Peter 2:5).

We are hidden in Christ (Col. 3:3).

We are justified in His sight without works (Rom. 3:28).

We are kept for Jesus Christ (Jude 1).

Life eternal is given to us by Jesus (John 10:28).

We are near to God by the blood of His Son (Eph. 2:13).

We are ordained to eternal life (Acts 13:48).

We have peace with God (Rom. 5:1).

We are quickened together with Christ (Eph. 2:5).

We are redeemed to God by Christ's blood (Rev. 5:9).

ALL OF THESE BLESSINGS ARE THE RESULT

OF GRACE!

I cannot but say, "Thanks be unto God for His unspeakable gift!"

GALATIANS -- CHAPTER FIVE

1. Stand fast therefore in the liberty wherewith Christ hath made us free, and be not entangled again with the yoke of bondage.
2. Behold, I Paul say unto you, that if ye be circumcised, Christ shall profit you nothing.
3. For I testify again to every man that is circumcised, that he is a debtor to do the whole law.
4. Christ is become of no effect unto you, whosoever of you are justified by the law; ye are fallen from grace.
5. For we through the Spirit wait for the hope of righteousness by faith.
6. For in Jesus Christ neither circumcision availeth any thing, nor uncircumcision; but faith which worketh by love.
7. Ye did run well; who did hinder you that ye should not obey the truth?
8. This persuasion cometh not of him that calleth you.
9. A little leaven leaveneth the whole lump.
10. I have confidence in you through the Lord, that ye will be none otherwise minded: but he that troubleth you shall bear his judgment, whosoever he be.
11. And I, brethren, if I yet preach circumcision, why do I yet suffer persecution? then is the offence of the cross ceased.
12. I would they were even cut off which trouble you.
13. For, brethren, ye have been called unto liberty; only use not liberty for an occasion to the flesh, but by love serve one another.
14. For all the law is fulfilled in one word, even in this; Thou shalt love thy neighbour as thyself.
15. But if ye bite and devour one another, take heed that ye be not consumed one of another.
16. This I say then, Walk in the Spirit, and ye shall not fulfil the lust of the flesh.
17. For the flesh lusteth against the Spirit, and the Spirit against the flesh: and these are contrary the one to the other: so that ye cannot do the things that ye would.
18. But if ye be led of the Spirit, ye are not under the law.
19. Now the works of the flesh are manifest, which are these; Adultery, fornication, uncleanness, lasciviousness,
20. Idolatry, witchcraft, hatred, variance, emulations, wrath, strife, seditions, heresies,
21. Envyings, murders, drunkenness, revellings, and such like: of the which I tell you before, as I have also told you in time past, that they which do such things shall not inherit the kingdom of God.
22. But the fruit of the Spirit is love, joy, peace, longsuffering, gentleness, goodness, faith,
23. Meekness, temperance: against such there is no law.

24. And they that are Christ's have crucified the flesh with the affections and lusts.

25. If we live in the Spirit, let us also walk in the Spirit.

26. Let us not be desirous of vain glory, provoking one another, envying one another.

The fifth chapter of Galatians begins the application of doctrinal truths set forth in the first four chapters. Paul leaves no stone unturned in his attempt to show the Galatians the folly and foolishness of being led about by false teachers, legalizers, and mixers of Law and Grace. He did everything in his power, as the Holy Ghost dictated to him, to point out that the person who is *saved* by Grace is *kept* by Grace. Jesus is not only the author ——He is also the finisher of our faith. He is not only the Alpha, but also the Omega . . . and everything *between* the A and Z. Paul sums it up thus: "Ye are complete in Him" (Col. 2:10).

The message thus far in the first four chapters of Galatians is the message of salvation by Grace, justification by Grace, victory by Grace——and in the end, final salvation of soul, body and spirit——by Grace. Paul boldly declares the believer to be free from the Law (Rom. 8:2); the believer is dead to the Law (Gal. 2:19); the believer is delivered from the Law (Rom. 7:6); and Paul clearly declares, "CHRIST IS THE END OF THE LAW FOR RIGHTEOUSNESS TO EVERYONE THAT BELIEVETH" (Rom. 10:4). He brings the message of the first four chapters to a close by saying, "CAST OUT THE BONDWOMAN AND HER SON . . . so then, brethren, we are not children of the bondwoman (the Law) but of the free (children of Grace)" (Gal. 4:30–31).

He opens chapter five with these tremendous, precious words: "STAND FAST THEREFORE IN THE LIBERTY WHEREWITH CHRIST HATH MADE US FREE, and be not entangled again with the yoke of bondage."

Notice the last word of the doctrinal section of the Epistle to the Galatians: "Free!" The believer is *free* . . . he is set at liberty. The believer is delivered by the Deliverer, the Lord Jesus Christ, who conquered the world, the flesh and the devil, hell and the grave. Salvation by the marvelous Grace of God means deliverance and freedom. There is no bondage in Grace:

"If the Son therefore shall make you free, ye shall be free indeed" (John 8:36).

"Ye shall know the truth, and the truth shall make you free" (John 8:32).

Someone is probably saying, "Mr. Greene, it seems that would cause loose living. Seemingly you are permitting a license to sin." You are dead wrong!

"As many as are led by the Spirit of God, they are the sons of God" (Rom. 8:14).

"The Lord is my Shepherd . . . He leadeth me in the paths of righteousness for His name's sake" (Psalm 23).

The Holy Ghost leads the believer into the paths of right living. God never gave any man a permit to sin, and the preaching of pure Grace does not license believers to sin. The truly born-again child of God does not crave the beggarly elements of the world. We are free indeed . . . not free to sin, but free to serve the Lord Jesus from the heart, because of love——not because of fear, commandments, and compulsion. God does not compel sons to serve the Saviour. The sons of God serve Him because they love Him. We love Him because He first loved us. The believer is dead to the Law——but alive unto God.

Notice the words of Galatians 5:1: *"Stand fast there-*

fore in the liberty wherewith Christ hath made us free." Paul is simply saying here: "Stand fast, be firm, do not surrender one mite, one iota, of your liberty!"

I have been traveling for more than twenty-eight years in evangelistic work. I have been in churches that are supposed to be fundamental Bible churches, but beloved, the poor members there are under Law. They are bound to a little group of selfish, self-centered people who shout long and loud about the Grace of God, and then submit to the commands and the demands of the denomination or the fellowship to which they belong! Some Christians shout, "Independent! Unaffiliated!" But when you dig below the surface you find they are not independent; they have a machine of their own, and the minister dictates to and commands the members. According to the New Testament, born again believers are led by the Holy Ghost, not by the preacher in the pulpit. The preacher is the overseer, the leader——but he is not to command. He is to lead, and not to be "lord over God's heritage." He is to be "an example to the flock." Every true minister is the under-shepherd of the Lord.

The admonition given in Galatians 5:1 was needed by those to whom Paul was writing. Many of the believers there were tempted to return to Law in order to avoid persecution and the loss of members of their family and friends. They were being accused of being lawless . . . law-breakers, guilty of making the Grace of God an occasion (a license, a permit) to commit sin; but in spite of the accusations hurled at them, Paul admonished them to "STAND FAST! Do not compromise to keep the friendship of your family, your friends, or your fellow believers. Stand fast in the liberty you have received in the Grace of God. Do not go back to the yoke of bondage from which you have been set free!"

Verses 2–6: "Behold, I Paul say unto you, that if

ye be circumcised, Christ shall profit you nothing. For I testify again to every man that is circumcised, that he is a debtor to do the whole Law. Christ is become of no effect unto you, whosoever of you are justified by the Law; YE ARE FALLEN FROM GRACE. For we through the Spirit wait for the hope of righteousness by faith. For in Jesus Christ neither circumcision availeth any thing, nor uncircumcision; but faith which worketh by love."

The legalizers and Judaizers——the teachers who had come along behind Paul——insisted that the Gentiles must become Jews and submit to the rite of circumcision according to the Law of Moses, in order to be saved. Paul opposes this preaching and declares boldly, "If you Galatians submit to circumcision after the Law of Moses, you become debtor to do the whole Law and you are under the curse and condemnation of the Law! Christ then can profit you nothing. If you turn to circumcision as a part of salvation, then you are under the Law, debtor to the whole Law!"

Paul preached, "You cannot be saved by Law AND Grace. You are either saved by Law, or by Grace . . . there can be no mixture of the two. It must be all of Grace, or it is not Grace at all. If you look to the Law for justification, you totally miss the Grace of God and the liberty it brings. If you turn to circumcision as a part of your salvation, Christ is become of no effect unto you. Whosoever of you Galatians are justified——or seek to be justified——by the Law of Moses, you are fallen from Grace!" . . . . . . Well! Someone is saying, "Mr. Greene, do you really admit that it is possible to fall from grace?"

According to the Scripture I have just read, there is such a thing as falling from Grace! But what is the meaning of this expression, "Ye are fallen from grace?" There are many denominations (and tens of thousands of church members and preachers) who teach that one who has been truly born again, truly washed in the blood, truly saved by the Grace of God, can fall from Grace, completely lose his salvation and his position in Grace ——and burn in hell forever. They tell us that when a Christian ceases to work and live the testimony of Grace, that person has fallen *from* Grace.

I am not discussing the doctrine of falling from Grace, or "once saved always saved," as some refer to eternal life. What I want to point out here is the truth that Paul is attempting to get across to the Galatians who are trying to mix Law and Grace. It may be interesting to you to know that this is the only place in the Word of God where the term "Ye are fallen from Grace" is used . . . or any term like unto this one having to do with falling from Grace. Here we learn that the moment a believer begins to work, to try to keep the Law or to be circumcised in order to keep himself saved, that person has fallen from Grace. The harder a person works to be saved or to keep saved, the further from Grace that person has fallen. It is utterly impossible to mix works with redemption. It is possible for a believer to fall from Grace, but it is *not* possible for a believer to fall from *sonship* if the believer is truly born into the family of God, is truly a son of God through the application of the blood of Jesus to the heart. God saves us through the power of the blood, covers us with the blood——and *keeps* us by the *power of the blood*. The whole process is by Grace through faith plus nothing.

I preach with all my heart that a Christian should do all the good, perform all the good works, he possibly can. A Christian should not be unfruitful (read Titus 3:14). We should bear fruit, more fruit, much fruit. We should not be satisfied with thirty-fold, or sixty-fold. We should strive for a hundred-fold . . . and according to I Corinthians 3:11—15 it is possible for a born again son of God to enter God's heaven and completely lose his reward! Works do not save us, works do not help to save us; works do not keep us saved, works do not help to keep us saved. From the beginning to the end of a true experience with God, it is all Grace plus nothing. "AND IF BY GRACE, THEN IS IT NO MORE OF WORKS: OTHERWISE GRACE IS NO MORE GRACE. BUT IF IT BE OF WORKS, THEN IT IS NO MORE GRACE: OTHERWISE WORK IS NO MORE WORK" (Rom. 11:6).

If there is any one thing that is clear and understandable in the New Testament, it is the fact that Law and Grace do not mix . . . cannot mix. It is all of Grace ——one hundred percent Grace——*plus nothing.*

I know someone is asking the question, "What happens to a believer who thus falls from Grace and returns to Law or works for justification?" The answer is very clearly stated in verse 4: "CHRIST IS BECOME OF NO EFFECT UNTO YOU, WHOSOEVER OF YOU ARE JUSTIFIED BY THE LAW; YE ARE FALLEN FROM GRACE." What the literal Greek language says here is simply, "Ye are severed from Christ. Ye who would be justified by the Law, ye are fallen away from Grace." The Greek expression translated by the Authorized Version as "become of no effect" is translated in the Revised Version (NOT the Revised Standard Version, but the Revised Version) as "severed . . . or brought to naught." The same expression is used by Paul in Romans 7:2 where the Authorized Version translates it "loosed" and the Revised Version translates it "discharged." Read Romans 7:6. The effect of such loosing (discharging) or severing from Christ has nothing to do with sonship. What is meant is simply that during the time the believer is practicing Law, Christ becomes of no experimental effect. The believer's position in Christ has not changed, but the believer's liberty is lost and therefore his joy is lost. And if the believer continues in this state, the *reward* will be lost. Salvation is by Grace through faith . . . totally and entirely independent of good works; therefore the believer as a born again son cannot be severed from Christ, loosed from Christ, or discharged from God's family; but the believer's fellowship can be interrupted, his testimony can be hindered, his reward can be lost, his joy can cease . . . and he can become unfruitful. That is the reason this precious old Book admonishes the little, tender children of God in these words: "MY LITTLE CHILDREN (not little sinners, or little backsliders, or little fallen-from-Grace folks) THESE THINGS WRITE I UNTO YOU (my little children) THAT YE (my little children) SIN NOT. AND IF ANY MAN SIN (any one of my sons) WE (John the Beloved, and all of the beloved little children of God) HAVE AN ADVOCATE WITH THE FATHER, JESUS CHRIST THE RIGHTEOUS (that is the Lord Jesus who was holy, pure, undefiled, untouched by iniquity, no guile in Him . . . the righteous One, God in flesh, God's purity and holiness): AND HE (God's holy One, God's just One, God's only begotten, virgin-born Son, Jesus) IS THE PROPITIATION FOR OUR SINS (the sins of the precious, tender little children): AND NOT FOR OURS ONLY (that is, Jesus not only died and atoned for the sins of the little children), BUT ALSO FOR THE SINS OF THE WHOLE WORLD (Jesus died to save "whosoever will," regardless of color, class, or creed)" (I John 2:1–2).

Beloved, Grace does not give a license to sin; Grace does not give a license to practice sin; but "If we say that we have not sinned, we make Him a liar, and His word is not in us" (I John 1:10). These words are spoken to the little children. The entire first Epistle of John was dictated to John the Beloved by the Holy Ghost, that we might enjoy our spiritual birthright——and our spiritual birthright is *full joy*: "AND THESE THINGS WRITE WE UNTO YOU, THAT YOUR JOY MAY BE FULL" (I John 1:4). I am so glad the God I serve, the God I love, the God I have trusted all these years does not kick me out and damn me when I stumble . . . when I falter and fail. You might as well face it——failure to do all that you do to the glory of God is sin, because the Bible clearly states, "WHATSOEVER IS NOT OF FAITH IS SIN . . . . TO HIM THAT KNOWETH TO DO GOOD AND DOETH IT NOT, TO HIM IT IS SIN." The Grace of God does not license us to sin, but the Grace of God takes care of the believer (the little child) if he *does* sin. Hallelujah! What a Saviour! I have been saved over twenty-eight years and I have never entertained the thought or the desire to return to the beggarly elements of the world and the things of the devil. Truly born again children of God do not crave the hog pens of the world, the cesspools of iniquity, and the ungodly lusts of the damned. Set your affection on things above. Look up! Jesus sits on the right hand of God the Father! "Turn your eyes upon Jesus, look full in His wonderful face; and the things of earth will grow strangely dim in the light of His glory and Grace."

If the believer refuses to confess his sins and refuses to judge himself, then he will be dealt with by the chastening hand of Almighty God . . . and a believer *can* commit "the sin unto death." Paul warns, "For this cause many are weak and sickly among you, and many sleep. For if we would judge ourselves, we should not be judged. But when we are judged, we are chastened of the Lord, that we should not be condemned with the world" (I Cor. 11:30–32).

"For whom the Lord loveth He chasteneth, and scourgeth EVERY SON WHOM HE RECEIVETH. If ye endure chastening, God dealeth with you as with sons; for what son is he whom the Father chasteneth not? BUT IF YE BE WITHOUT CHASTISEMENT, WHEREOF ALL ARE PARTAKERS, THEN ARE YE BASTARDS, AND NOT SONS" (Heb. 12:6–8). I do not believe I need make any remarks concerning that passage––it is self-explanatory, very easily understood. A person who can practice sin, live in sin, enjoy sin and prosper therein without the chastening hand of God upon him, has never been truly born into God's Grace by the power of the blood of Jesus Christ. To join a church, to be baptized and live a good life for awhile, does not mean a person has been saved. Who has been saved and who has not been saved is known only by God Almighty. You may say, "I KNOW Preacher Greene is saved," and I may say of some person, "I KNOW that person is saved." But in reality you do not know, I do not know. All we can know of another person is what we see on the outside; but God Almighty looks on the heart.

I have two boys. They are young men now, but when they were just little lads I chastened them with a switch, with my belt, and in other ways. I did it because I loved them, not because I hated them. I chastened them because I was their friend, not their enemy. God chastens every child He has; and any person who claims to be a Christian but has not been chastened of the Lord is a spiritual illegitimate . . . he has never been born into God's family, according to Paul and the dictation of the Holy Ghost through his pen! Do not get angry with me for what I have said––I have simply pointed out Hebrews

12:6—8. I did not write it; I am just preaching it. God did not ask my permission to put that passage in the Bible. It was put there because it is truth . . . "Ye shall know the truth, and the truth shall make you free!" Therefore, stand fast in the liberty of the marvelous Grace of our God!

In Corinth, Christians died under the chastening hand of God while out of fellowship . . . and yet, the Holy Ghost said, "But when we are judged, we are chastened of the Lord, that we should not be condemned with the world!" That is what the Holy Ghost said through the pen of Paul. They were chastened of the Lord that they should not be condemned. Condemnation to a Christian is impossible. God, through chastening, brings the Christian to his knees in tears. Peter wept bitterly when he saw the tender eyes of Jesus looking his way after he had denied Him, after he had even cursed and sworn that he did not know Him! Praise God for Grace!

Paul testifying for himself and all believers, says in verse 5:

"We through the Spirit wait for the hope of righteousness by faith." The believer's hope is in the Holy Ghost of God, and it is by faith. Please note: "By faith!"

In Jesus, circumcision does not avail anything. Uncircumcision does not avail anything; but faith is the key, the heart, the soul, the life, the essence of salvation. "Faith worketh by love." Salvation does not come through circumcision, baptism, confirmation, ceremony, joining the church, turning over a new leaf, doing the best you can, living a good life, being honest and upright. Salvation comes *by faith alone*. Faith that saves is ours only by hearing the Word of God, and faith which is living faith . . . saving faith . . . does not abide alone. Faith which saves will do more than save. Fire which smokes, *burns* as well as produces smoke. Faith which saves produces works . . . the work of love. The salvation we enjoy through faith is without works——but faith which does not work is dead faith. Living faith produces works. Study carefully Ephesians 2:8–10 and James 2:17–20.

Verse 7: "Ye did run well; who did hinder you that ye should not obey the truth?" The Galatians had begun in the Spirit——and they were now trying to be made perfect and become holy by the works of the flesh. Paul declared that an enemy had given them this idea.

Verse 8: "This persuasion cometh not of Him that calleth you." What Paul is saying here is simply this: "You Galatians may rest assured that God has had nothing to do with your deviating from His Grace and turning to legalistic practices. The enemy has done this!"

Verse 9: "A little leaven leaveneth the whole lump." No doubt Paul is referring here to the parable of the leaven in Matthew 13:33. It is alarming, it is amazing, and very strange that many Bible teachers teach that leaven is a symbol of the Gospel which is to be mixed in the world until finally the Gospel will bring the whole world to salvation and thus the whole lump will be leavened and we will have Utopia——a kingdom of righteousness on earth. There is no Scriptural ground for such a doctrine. There is no excuse for such ignorance! Any person with a good Bible concordance can study "leaven" in the Word of God. Leaven is always mentioned in the Old Testament in an evil sense. Read Genesis 19:3, and study the references given there. In the New Testament the symbolic meaning of leaven is explained. According to the words of Jesus, leaven is "malice and wickedness," as contrasted with "sincerity and truth" (I Cor. 5:6–8). Leaven is evil doctrine (Matt. 16:12). Jesus referred to the leaven of the Pharisees, the Sadducees and the Herodians (Matt. 16:6; Mark 8:15). The leaven of the Pharisees was their practice of religious externalism (Matt. 23:14; Matt. 16:23—28). Leaven to the Sadducees was skepticism as to the supernatural teaching in Scripture . . . they did not believe in spirit or angel . . . they did not believe in a resurrection (Matt. 22:23—29). Leaven referring to the Herodians meant worldliness (Matt. 22:16—21; Mark 3:6). Paul uses the term two times: "A little leaven leaveneth the whole lump." In Galatians, leaven refers to the false doctrine of legalism——the mixing of Law and Grace. Writing to the believers at Corinth, in I Corinthians 5:6, it refers to immorality in personal life, which, continually tolerated by the Corinthian church, was a dangerous thing for the whole church. What Paul is saying to the Galatians in our present verse is simply this:

"Your legalistic seducers are not great in number . . . but there are enough of them to corrupt your whole church in Galatia. Circumcision is only a very small part of the Law——but if you practice circumcision in connection with salvation, then you have practiced enough Law to place you altogether under the legal yoke of bondage!" Paul did not pull any punches or soft-pedal his stern warning to the Galatians concerning the leaven of the legalizers. God help us today to be preachers like Paul!

Verse 10: "I have confidence in you through the Lord, that ye will be none otherwise minded: but he that troubleth you shall bear his judgment, whosoever he be." Paul warns that the legalizers will not get by with sowing tares and placing leaven in the assembly at Galatia. Whosoever he be, let him remember his judgment is double anathema. Read again Galatians 1:8—9. The end of these trouble makers, tare-sowers, and leaven-planters "SHALL

BE ACCORDING TO THEIR WORKS" (II Cor. 11:15). The dirtiest gang of thieves this side of hell is the gang of preachers who deviate from the Word of God and preach a gospel of their own choosing . . . a gospel to please parishioners who refuse to be born again according to the Bible formula. A gangster in the natural sense steals your money or your jewels. You can get more money and buy more jewels. But a lying preacher will steal your right to heaven . . . and if you die and go to hell you will never have another chance to enter heaven. Therefore, I say the dirtiest gang of thieves this side of hell is a gang of preachers who refuse to preach salvation by grace through faith in the shed blood of Jesus Christ--plus nothing!

Verse 11: "And I, brethren, if I yet preach circumcision, why do I yet suffer persecution? then is the offence of the cross ceased." You recall earlier in the ministry of Paul, for reasons known to Paul and to his God, he permitted Timothy to be circumcised and to practice certain Jewish observances. Read Acts 20:6 and Acts 21:34. It could be that because of this some of the Galatians brought the accusation against Paul. They accused him of preaching circumcision among the Jews, and then preaching against circumcision when he was among the Gentiles. This was a false accusation. Listen to Paul's own testimony:

"For though I be free from all men, yet have I made myself servant unto all, that I might gain the more. And unto the Jews I became as a Jew, that I might gain the Jews; to them that are under the Law, as under the Law, that I might gain them that are under the Law; To them that are without Law, as without Law, (being not without Law to God, but under the Law to Christ,) that I might gain them that are without Law; To the weak became I as weak, that I might gain the weak: I am made all things to all men, that I might by all means save some. AND THIS I DO FOR THE GOSPEL'S SAKE, THAT I MIGHT BE PARTAKER THEREOF WITH YOU" (I Cor. 9:19–23).

Yes, Paul indeed circumcised Timothy. He did it in order that Timothy might be more useful in reaching the Jews; but when Paul visited Jerusalem (according to the account given in Acts 15) and it was demanded that Titus, a Gentile, be circumcised as a condition of fellowship with the other apostles, Paul flatly refused in order that the "TRUTH OF THE GOSPEL MIGHT CONTINUE WITH YOU" (Gal. 2:5).

There has been only one Paul . . . there will never be another. I believe Paul did everything he did with a sincere heart, totally and entirely dedicated to the cause of the Gospel. I do not believe he ever willingly did anything that was out of the will of God. I believe he told the truth when he said, "I have fought a good fight, I have finished my course, I have kept the faith . . . I am now ready to be offered!"

In verse 11 Paul clears himself from the accusation that had been made against him: "If I yet preach circumcision, why do I yet suffer persecution? Then is the offence of the cross ceased." What he is saying is simply this: "If I preach to please people, then why am I persecuted?" Certainly they knew he had been persecuted ––stoned and dragged outside the city of Lystra for dead. He had been beaten and in prison. No man except the man Christ Jesus ever suffered more physical pain than Paul. The Galatians knew this, and they knew down deep in their hearts that Paul was not preaching to please men. They knew his message was "God forbid that I should glory save in the cross!" Paul preached Jesus Christ ––crucified, buried, risen, coming again "according to the Scriptures."

I like verse 12: "I WOULD THEY WERE EVEN CUT OFF WHICH TROUBLE YOU." I wish some of the educated, polished theologians would use that text next Sunday morning! There are brethren (so-called) who declare that the need of the world is for all religions to get together and have a great world council of churches —and bring in the Kingdom. I wish when this great world council of churches assembles, the Apostle Paul could step on the platform and preach for fifteen minutes! (He would preach the last twelve minutes to an empty house ——because the doctors would be gone!) They would not listen to his message . . . they would not endure it, they would not stand it. They would brand him as a fanatic, a crackpot and a fool. To the Galatian believers who had been confused and frustrated by a group of teachers who commanded the believers to be circumcised after the custom of the Law of Moses, Paul said: "I wish that crowd would die!"

That may be a little bit rough——but there is not much you can do about it. I did not write it——I am just reading it. Paul said, "I WOULD THEY WERE EVEN CUT OFF WHICH TROUBLE YOU!! I came here and preached the Grace of God, you accepted the Grace of God, you were born into the Grace of God, you have enjoyed the liberty of the Grace of God; and now these legalizers and Judaizers come along and command you to be circumcised after the Law of Moses! I wish they were dead . . . I wish they were cut off!"

Verse 13: "For, brethren, ye have been called unto liberty; only use not liberty for an occasion to the flesh, but by love serve one another."

In this verse Paul is saying to the Galatians the same thing he said to the Romans in Romans 14:1–15:3. Read that passage carefully. Paul said the same thing to the believers at Corinth in I Corinthians 8:1–13. To these churches, to the believers, Paul is saying, "Brethren, you have been called to freedom . . . liberty; only, make not your freedom grounds to satisfy the flesh—— but rather enslave yourselves one to another by the bondage of fervent love!"

A born again man, walking in the light as Jesus is in the light (I John 1:7), walking in fellowship with the Father and His Son Jesus Christ (I John 1:3–4) will never use his freedom from the Law as an opening to sin. He will never use that freedom to deliver him from the obligation of living a holy, righteous, godly life. The Grace of God which brings this liberty teaches us to deny ungodliness and worldly lusts, and to live soberly, righteously, and godly in this present world, looking for that blessed hope and the glorious appearing of the great God and our Saviour Jesus Christ (Titus 2:11–15). The believer is indeed free from the Law; but the love of Christ in the heart of the believer constrains him to live blameless, pure, upright.

"What shall we say then? Shall we continue in sin, that grace may abound? God forbid!" Read Romans 6: 1–15. Shall we continue in sin because we are not under the Law of Moses——but under the Grace of God? God forbid! No, we shall not.

Verse 14: "For all the Law is fulfilled in one word, even in this: THOU SHALT LOVE THY NEIGHBOUR AS THYSELF." The verse is clear, understandable, self-explanatory.

Verse 15: "But if ye bite and devour one another, take heed that ye be not consumed one of another."

I sometimes use this verse when preaching to believers on the subject of "Cannibal Christians." Churches devour themselves by fussing and back-biting because of jealousy, envy and strife. Instead of being child*like* in faith and practice, they are child*ish*, acting like children fussing in the sandbox in the back yard! Churches often devour themselves——they devour each other——as a result of disturbances within the church over petty doctrines. Whichever side wins keeps the building, the other crowd moves out and starts a new building program——and in reality both sides lose . . . no one gains, reproach is brought on the church. I believe we should come out from liberals and modernists, but Paul is speaking here to born again believers who are being confused and frustrated by legalistic preachers. If these believers begin to bite and devour one another, they will be consumed of each other . . . which is what the devil wanted. That is the reason Paul gives warning against such living.

VICTORY OVER SIN
COMES THROUGH THE HOLY SPIRIT

Verses 16 and 17: "This I say then, Walk in the Spirit, and ye shall not fulfil the lust of the flesh. For the flesh lusteth against the Spirit, and the Spirit against the flesh: and these things are contrary the one to the other: so that ye cannot do the things that ye would."

Someone may be asking, "What is the lust of the flesh?" The answer is, *The lust of the flesh is any kind of selfish, fleshly desire.* The great problem in the life of most Christians is how to avoid selfish living . . . how to be victorious over selfish desires. The answer is clearly stated here: *"Walk in the Spirit."* If we walk by the Holy Spirit, if we are led by the Holy Spirit, if we yield ourselves to the Holy Spirit, if we present our bodies a living sacrifice, holy and acceptable unto God in the Holy Spirit and give the Holy Spirit right of way in our lives, He will give us victory over our selfish, lustful desires.

There is much ignorance among God's people concerning our relationship, as believers, to the Holy Spirit. I think it would be to our advantage to stop here and point out a few things concerning this relationship:

First of all, every saved person——every person who is a recipient of God's Grace——is born of the Holy Ghost, and through the power of the Holy Ghost becomes a child of God. Study John's Gospel 3:3—8, James 1:18, I Peter 1:22, I Peter 2:3.

In the second place, the moment a person is born again, that child of God is baptized in the Holy Ghost into the body of Christ, and through the baptism of the Holy Ghost becomes a member of the body of Christ—— of His flesh and of His bones. Study carefully I Corinthians 12:12—15, Ephesians 4:4, Ephesians 5:30. The baptism of the Spirit described in I Corinthians 12:12 is the only baptism of the Holy Ghost known to Scripture. The Lord Jesus Christ is the One who is the baptizer. Read Matthew 3:11; read Acts 1:5.

In the third place, the moment the new birth is experienced, that child of God receives the Holy Ghost in his heart (Rom. 8:9, Rom. 8:14). The Holy Spirit is the unction, the anointing, the teacher. He guards the believer from the danger of apostasy. Study carefully I John 2:18—27.

In the fourth place, every born again child of God is sealed by (or in) the Holy Ghost the moment he receives the new birth . . . and is thus made God's son, sealed until the day of redemption when our Lord returns. Study carefully II Cor. 1:21—22, Eph. 1:13—14, Eph. 4:30.

In the fifth place, every born again child of God receives the Holy Ghost as the indwelling presence of Almighty God the moment that person is born again. The

Holy Ghost--the Third Person of the Trinity--abides continually every second of every minute, every hour of every day, in the heart of the born again one (I Cor. 3:16, I Cor. 6:19-20).

In the sixth place, every born again child of God should be--and CAN be--filled with the Holy Spirit. When the born again one is filled with the Holy Spirit he will *walk* by the Spirit, and he will not fulfill the lusts of the flesh. Study Ephesians 5:18-21, Romans 8:8-11, Romans 12:1-2.

Last, but by no means least, the Holy Ghost helps every believer in his prayer life: "Likewise the Spirit also helpeth our infirmities: for we know not what we should pray for as we ought: but the Spirit itself maketh intercession for us with groanings which cannot be uttered. And He (the Holy Spirit) that searcheth the hearts knoweth what is the mind of the Spirit, because He maketh intercession for the saints according to the will of God" (Rom. 8:26-27). Thank God for the Holy Spirit!

Verses 17-21: "For the flesh lusteth against the Spirit, and the Spirit against the flesh: and these are contrary the one to the other: so that ye cannot do the things that ye would. But if ye be led of the Spirit, ye are not under the Law. Now the works of the flesh are manifest, which are these; Adultery, fornication, uncleanness, lasciviousness, idolatry, witchcraft, hatred, variance, emulations, wrath, strife, seditions, heresies, envyings, murders, drunkenness, revellings, and such like: of the which I tell you before, as I have also told you in time past, that they which do such things shall not inherit the kingdom of God."

Verse 17 tells us that the flesh "lusteth against the Spirit, and the Spirit against the flesh." The Spirit and the flesh do not agree, these are contrary one to the other, so that we cannot do the things we would. That is, we cannot follow the desire of the flesh, we cannot do the things the flesh suggests. It will be a happy, victorious day in the lives of many Christians when they recognize the *two natures* of a believer. When we are unbelievers there is only *one* nature--the sinful nature; but when the Holy Ghost moves into our heart, then there is a new life in the heart. That which is born of the flesh is flesh, and that which is born of the Spirit is spirit. When God Almighty saves a sinner, God saves the *spirit*, the heart, the inner man; the *flesh* is destined to return to the dust. And regardless of how holy, sanctified and dedicated you may be, you will never cease to live on this earth in a body of flesh. You had better recognize that fact. Paul warns, "Let him that thinketh he standeth take heed lest he fall" (I Cor. 10:12). Yes, the Spirit and the flesh do not agree, they are contrary the one to the other.

"But if ye be led of the Spirit ye are not under the Law." That is, if you are led of the Spirit, you cannot be led by the Law! If you are led by the Spirit, you are not under the Law, because the Spirit is in the world to glorify Jesus, to speak of Jesus--and Jesus is the Author of Grace. Therefore, you cannot be led of the Spirit and be under Law at the same time!

Beginning with verse 19, Paul gives a sordid list of the works of the flesh. I do not feel it necessary to use time and space to enlarge upon what the Holy Ghost tells us through the pen of the Apostle to the Gentiles. He clearly states the works of the flesh--and there is no way to misunderstand: Adultery, fornication, uncleanness, lasciviousness, idolatry, witchcraft, hatred, variance, emulations, wrath, strife, seditions, heresies, envyings, murders, drunkenness, revellings, and such like . . . "and such like" . . . that is, anything else like these just named. Paul says, "I have told you before, I am repeating, they which do such things shall not in any case, under any circumstances, enter the kingdom of God!" I have often made the statement in my meetings that if some folks did get to Heaven, Heaven would become hell five minutes after they arrived! You weigh that statement before you criticize it, and I believe you will agree with me. You need not worry about the adulterers, adulteresses, the idolators, witchcraft workers, those who hate, who murder, those who envy and those who get drunk. They will not be in that number when the saints go marching in. They will be screaming in the pit, in the lake of fire. Paul here is *not* referring to backslidden believers. He is referring to people who have never been born again. He gives the same warning to the believers in the church at Corinth:

"Know ye not that the unrighteous shall not inherit the kingdom of God? Be not deceived: neither fornicators, nor idolaters, nor adulterers, nor effeminate, nor abusers of themselves with mankind, nor thieves, nor covetous, nor drunkards, nor revilers, nor extortioners, shall inherit the kingdom of God. And such were some of you: but ye are washed, but ye are sanctified, but ye are justified in the name of the Lord Jesus, and by the Spirit of our God" (I Cor. 6:9—11). Al! born again believers are washed in the blood, sanctified by the blood, justified by the blood. Of course, the catalog of sins named in our present Scripture as the works of the flesh are not characteristic in the lives of born again, bloodwashed, redeemed Christians. Read I Cor. 1:29—30.

THE FRUIT OF THE SPIRIT

In the next two verses Paul gives to us a catalog of the fruit of the Spirit. He has just named the works of the flesh, and now he gives to us the bright picture

. . . the Holy Spirit's fruit-basket:

Verses 22 and 23: "But the fruit of the Spirit is love, joy, peace, longsuffering, gentleness, goodness, faith, meekness, temperance: against such there is no law."

Please note: "BUT THE FRUIT OF THE SPIRIT IS . . . ." Please observe, pay attention: These good things are referred to as "fruit," *not works*! Not one of the Spirit-fruit named here can be bought, earned, secured through human effort. No matter how much we try to do good, be good, live good, we will fail to bear the fruit of the Spirit. We cannot love as we ought to love, by *trying* to love. It is easy to love the lovely, those who are always doing and saying kind things about us; but Christian love loves the unlovely. Joy cannot be brought to the human heart by doing; money cannot buy joy; peace cannot be purchased. Jesus said, "My peace I leave with you, My peace I give unto you" (John 14:27). Jesus said, "Come unto me, all ye that labor and are heavy-laden and I will give you rest" (Matt. 11:28). Peace and rest are God's gifts.

Longsuffering is a grace produced only by the Holy Spirit. To be gentle and good, to have faith, to be meek, temperate . . . these things come through the Spirit. Before leaving these two verses, let me point out that the word is singular: FRUIT . . . (not "fruits" . . . plural). So——every born again child of God who is led by the Spirit should love, be filled with joy and peace; every true believer should be longsuffering, gentle, good. Every believer should have faith, every believer should be meek and temperate . . . and of course, against such living there is no law. I wonder if I bear the fruit of the Spirit? You might ask yourself the same question . . . and if we are not bearing fruit, then God help us to do something about it!

Verse 24: "And they that are Christ's have crucified the flesh with the affections and lusts." If you are having trouble with the flesh, I wish you would order my 32-page booklet on THE TWO NATURES. This booklet has helped thousands of believers in the last ten years. A moment ago I said––and I repeat––it will be a happy day in the lives of some Christians when they recognize that a believer has two natures––the flesh and the Spirit. We can, by the grace of God and by His power, crucify the flesh; but the flesh must be crucified daily. Again ––"Let him that thinketh he standeth take heed lest he fall!" But––"There hath no temptation taken you but such as is common to man: but God is faithful, who will not suffer you to be tempted above that ye are able; but will with the temptation also make a way to escape, that ye may be able to bear it" (I Cor. 10:13). If you do not already know that verse of Scripture from memory, *memorize it now*, before you read another paragraph!

Born again believers, they who are Christ's, have crucified the flesh with its passions and lusts. Believers have accepted the cross of the Lord Jesus. It is Christ whom the believer has put on by faith––therefore, with Paul we say, "I am crucified with Christ: nevertheless I live; yet not I, but Christ liveth in me: and the life which I now live in the flesh I live by the faith of the Son of God, who loved me, and gave Himself for me" (Gal. 2:20).

Verse 25: "If we live in the Spirit, let us also walk in the Spirit." That is, if we are born again, if we are born of the Spirit, if the Holy Spirit abides in our bosom, if God has honored us with the presence of the Third Person of the Trinity within us, then let us yield ourselves to Him––and let us give Him the right-of-way in our lives . . . in every minute detail of our living.

Verse 26: "Let us not be desirous of vain glory, provoking one another, envying one another."

The believers in the assembly at Galatia were in grave danger of quarreling among themselves, disputing among themselves concerning the Law, instead of worshipping the Christ who bought them with His blood. They needed this exhortation from the Apostle Paul. Of course, that danger did not cease with the Galatians . . . it still remains among Christians today! I am sure the Lord God looks down from Heaven many times with a sad heart, when churches spend their time arguing––splitting hairs over denominational questions––when they should be singing the praises of God and worshipping the Christ who redeemed them at the tremendous price of His blood on Calvary's cross. God help us as believers to walk in the Spirit, to be led by the Spirit–– and if we are led by the Spirit and walk in the Spirit we will not desire vain glory. We will not be envious of our fellow-believers. We will not provoke each other to sin. And when we assemble ourselves together, our one motive for assembling should be to worship in spirit and in truth the God who so loved us that He gave His only begotten Son, that WE might have life and have it abundantly–– by Grace, through faith in His finished work––plus nothing! *"Believe on the Lord Jesus Christ, and thou shalt be saved!"* Receive the Lord Jesus Christ and He will give to you the power to become a son of the living God!

GALATIANS — CHAPTER SIX

1. Brethren, if a man be overtaken in a fault, ye which are spiritual, restore such an one in the spirit of meekness; considering thyself, lest thou also be tempted.
2. Bear ye one another's burdens, and so fulfil the law of Christ.
3. For if a man think himself to be something, when he is nothing, he deceiveth himself.
4. But let every man prove his own work, and then shall he have rejoicing in himself alone, and not in another.
5. For every man shall bear his own burden.
6. Let him that is taught in the word communicate unto him that teacheth in all good things.
7. Be not deceived; God is not mocked: for whatsoever a man soweth, that shall he also reap.
8. For he that soweth to his flesh shall of the flesh reap corruption; but he that soweth to the Spirit shall of the Spirit reap life everlasting.
9. And let us not be weary in well doing: for in due season we shall reap, if we faint not.
10. As we have therefore opportunity, let us do good unto all men, especially unto them who are of the household of faith.
11. Ye see how large a letter I have written unto you with mine own hand.
12. As many as desire to make a fair shew in the flesh, they constrain you to be circumcised; only lest they should suffer persecution for the cross of Christ.
13. For neither they themselves who are circumcised keep the law; but desire to have you circumcised, that they may glory in your flesh.
14. But God forbid that I should glory, save in the cross of our Lord Jesus Christ, by whom the world is crucified unto me, and I unto the world.
15. For in Christ Jesus neither circumcision availeth any thing, nor uncircumcision, but a new creature.
16. And as many as walk according to this rule, peace be on them, and mercy, and upon the Israel of God.
17. From henceforth let no man trouble me: for I bear in my body the marks of the Lord Jesus.
18. Brethren, the grace of our Lord Jesus Christ be with your spirit. Amen.

In chapter 5, Paul gave to the Galatian believers a general view of the practical application of the doctrine of the marvelous Grace of God. He pointed out the evidence and proof of our justification by faith, without the works of the Law . . . *salvation by Grace through faith plus nothing*. He pointed out the difference between the legalist and the true born again believer. The legalizer measures a man by the Law––and naturally finds much to point out in his life that is wrong and brings condemnation; but the man who is saved by Grace and is living by Grace is gracious, and bears fruit described in the last part of chapter five.

Galatians 6:1: "Brethren, if a man be overtaken in a fault, ye which are spiritual, restore such an one in the spirit of meekness; considering thyself, lest thou also be tempted."

You may rest assured that a born again child of God should not heap judgment and damnation upon the head of a fellow-believer who has stumbled. A true believer knows that none of us are immune from temptation and sin until we get our glorified body when Jesus comes in the Rapture of the church. There are thousands of church people today who judge their fellow church members by the clothes they wear, the day they worship, the doctrines they hold in their particular organization. Grace does not emphasize days, rituals, or programs. A born again child of God will dress decently and will eat and drink things befitting a child of God. The Christian religion is not observing days and feasts, nor abstaining from meats, etc. A spiritually minded person will be slow to judge another Christian, because the closer we live to God, the more we realize how totally dependent we are upon Him for salvation and for victory over the world, the flesh, and the devil. I remind you again, "Let him that thinketh he standeth take heed lest he fall!" Hear these words: "For I know that in me (that is, in my flesh,) dwelleth no good thing" (Rom. 7:18a). Paul put no confidence in his flesh (read Phil. 3:3).

In the first verse of Galatians 6 Paul is speaking to

the "brethren" . . . believers, born again people. He is admonishing them concerning their treatment of a brother who has stumbled. They are not to judge him, condemn him and damn him; but they are to forgive him and restore him. The man who has stumbled does not need to be pushed down further——he needs to be lifted up. He does not need to be criticized and condemned. A brother who has fallen into sin needs help——not judgment. We dare not sit in judgment against our brother. The Lord God will judge all things at the appointed time. We do not know the circumstances which may have brought to pass the stumbling of a brother. If we faced the same temptation under the same conditions, we might do even worse than the one we are prone to criticize! If our brother in the Lord is overtaken in a fault, we should restore that brother and help him and encourage him. If we see a brother doing something not becoming to a Christian we should not announce it to the church, but we should attempt to help the brother. If we are spiritually minded, we will hear and obey Paul's admonition to the Corinthians: "Therefore judge nothing before the time, until the Lord come, who both will bring to light the hidden things of darkness, and will make manifest the counsels of the hearts: and then shall every man have praise of God" (I Cor. 4:5). Jesus alone knows the secret of each heart. He sees the motives of each heart, and He will take care of the judging of believers at the judgment seat of Christ when each of us will be rewarded for our faithful stewardship. It is much easier for some to live a victorious life than for others to do so. Some of you dear people reading these lines have never known sin——you have never dabbled in the world, have never tasted iniquity. Some of the rest of us drank the very dregs of wickedness. We face temptation of which you know nothing. Oh, yes——God is able . . . but do not forget that while the spirit is willing, the flesh is weak. We will be hounded by the flesh until we receive our glorified bodies.

The number-one desire of the devil is to damn you; but if you give your heart to Jesus and are saved by grace through faith, then the devil declares war on your influence and testimony. He does everything in his ungodly power to rob you of the joy of salvation, the victory of the power of God and the full reward that is your spiritual birthright at the end of a consecrated, dedicated, victorious spiritual life.

Verses 2—5: "Bear ye one another's burdens, and so fulfil the law of Christ. For if a man think himself to be something, when he is nothing, he deceiveth himself. But let every man prove his own work, and then shall he have rejoicing in himself alone, and not in another. For every man shall bear his own burden."

Paul was speaking to a group who were attempting to keep the Law. He said, "Here is the Law . . . for those of you who want to keep the Law and be under the Law. Bear ye one another's burdens and so fulfil the Law of Christ. Do not bite and devour one another, do not condemn and judge each other, do not fuss and fight over circumcision and rituals. If you want to practice the Law, then bear one another's burdens. Love one another, be at peace with one another. Be longsuffering and gentle. Be good, be meek, be kind . . . and temperate. Bear one another's burdens if you want to fulfil the Law of Christ. Love your neighbor just like you love yourself! Love Jesus with all your heart, soul, spirit, mind and strength, if you want to fulfil the Law!"

In verse 3 Paul attacks self-conceit. There is no place for conceit and pride in the Christian life. It is wonderful to know that we are saved by Grace, kept by the power of God, and that *in Jesus* we possess the fulness of the Godhead bodily, that we are complete in the Lord Jesus Christ. Read Colossians 2:9–10. But while we are praising God for these glorious facts in Grace, let it never be forgotten that in the flesh DWELLETH NO GOOD THING (Rom. 7:18). My brother and sister, if you do not commit your flesh to the Holy Ghost––unreservedly––the flesh will be your downfall spiritually! The devil will use the body in which you live to rob you of the joy and the victory, the assurance, peace and reward that your spiritual birthright guarantees! That is the reason Paul begged the believers at Rome to present their bodies a living sacrifice (Rom. 12:1–2).

In verses 4 and 5 Paul points out that even though we are commanded to bear one another's burdens, we must not forget our own burden . . . that is, "let every man prove his own work, and then shall he have rejoicing in himself alone and not in another, for every man must bear his own burden." There are burdens we can bear for others, or which we can help our fellow believer to bear. But there is a personal burden that we must bear, a burden which no one else can bear for us. Jesus said, "Take up the cross and follow Me." Jesus will do many things for you––but He will not carry for you the cross *you* should carry. Therefore, while we are helping others to bear their burdens, there is a responsibility that rests upon the individual because we are sons of God. We need to prove our own stewardship, our own work. We need to be careful in all that we do, "whether we eat or drink, or whatsoever we do," we should do it all to the glory of God.

Verse 6: "Let him that is taught in the Word communicate unto him that teacheth in all good things."

The word "communicate" used in this verse means "to share." Notice it is a command . . . not a suggestion.

It is addressed to those who receive help from teachers of the Word of God. The teachers of God's Word feed those who hear the Word; thereby, those who hear feed on the spiritual bread and the spiritual meat. The hearers are commanded to share with the teachers . . . that is, the material things, such as food, raiment and money. Read Romans 15:27. Paul wrote to the believers in the church at Corinth and said, "If we have sown unto you spiritual things, is it a great thing if we shall reap your carnal things? . . . even so hath the Lord ordained that they which preach the Gospel should live of the Gospel" (I Cor. 9:11–14).

I do not hesitate to say that it is a reflection on any church not to take care of their pastor. Let me explain: A new church just beginning might not be financially able to take care of a pastor, and the pastor might be forced to work for a season; but after the church has grown to seventy-five or a hundred members or more, it certainly should pay the pastor a living wage in order that he could spend his time ministering to the spiritual needs of the parishioners. The ministry of the Gospel is a full time job. I hate to say this––and yet, say it I must: Preaching is a side line with some ministers. They operate a business and preach on the side. I do not desire to hurt anyone, and the Bible says, "Touch not mine anointed" . . . but a minister of the Gospel who spends more time making money in the business world than he spends preaching the Gospel is using the Gospel as a side line! I repeat––to be the pastor of a church, or to be an evangelist, is a full time job––seven days a week, every hour of every day. So Paul commands the Galatians to share the carnal things with the spiritual leaders. "They that preach the Gospel shall live by the Gospel." Certainly, "The laborer is worthy of his hire." The reason so many Christians are so lean and barren spiritually is because they sow sparingly——therefore, they reap sparingly. But if we would sow bountifully, we would reap bountifully. God loves a cheerful giver.

Verses 7–9: "Be not deceived; God is not mocked: for whatsoever a man soweth, that shall he also reap. For he that soweth to his flesh shall of the flesh reap corruption; but he that soweth to the Spirit shall of the Spirit reap life everlasting. And let us not be weary in well doing: for in due season we shall reap, if we faint not."

I believe every verse of Scripture has a primary interpretation and application, and I believe it has a secondary application. Paul said in verse 6, "Let him that is taught in the Word communicate unto him that teacheth in all good things," and then uses the illustration of sowing and reaping (terms recognized everywhere). If we sow wheat seed, we reap wheat. If we sow oats, we reap oats. If we sow barley, we reap barley. If we sow corn, we reap corn. So it is in the spiritual realm: If we sow to the flesh——if we satisfy, pamper and pet the flesh, if we feed the flesh, if we spend on the flesh money that we should give to the work of the Lord, then we will reap corruption. But if we sow to the Spirit——if we give our time, talents, and money to further spiritual things, then we will of the Spirit reap life everlasting. I believe this Scripture goes deeper. A person who follows the flesh, lives for the satisfaction and pleasures of the flesh, will reap corruption in hell forever. Verse 9 declares that we should not be weary in well doing, for in due season we shall reap if we faint not. There is such a thing as losing your reward. In II John 7–8 we are warned, "For many deceivers are entered into the world, who confess not that Jesus Christ is come in the flesh. This is a deceiver and an antichrist. LOOK TO YOURSELVES (be careful, watch yourselves), THAT WE LOSE NOT THOSE

THINGS WHICH WE HAVE WROUGHT, BUT THAT WE RECEIVE A FULL REWARD." This has nothing to do with redemption or salvation of the soul. It is speaking of stewardship. Verses 9, 10 and 11 in the Epistle of II John warn us concerning those who preach any doctrine except the doctrine Jesus preached. If we bring these false teachers into our homes, if we give them money and bid them God speed, then we are partaker of their evil deeds and we will lose our reward. It will be a happy day in the lives of many Christians when they distinguish between redemption and reward . . . when they distinguish between salvation and stewardship. We are saved by Grace——but we are *rewarded* for our faithful labors. So we should not be weary in well doing, for we will reap eventually——that is, if we faint not. If we faint, we lose our reward. Read I Corinthians 3:11—15.

Verse 10: "As we have therefore opportunity, let us do good unto all men, especially unto them who are of the household of faith."

Read the seventeenth chapter of John carefully, and you will see that Jesus prayed for the believers, and His prayer is primarily in the interest of His children here on earth. We are to do good to all men——but we are to do good *especially* unto the household of faith . . . Christian brothers and sisters. John tells us the same thing in I John 3:16—19:

"Hereby perceive we the love of God, because He laid down His life for us: and we ought to lay down our lives for the brethren. But whoso hath this world's good, and seeth his brother have need, and shutteth up his bowels of compassion from him, how dwelleth the love of God in him? My little children, let us not love in word, neither in tongue; but in deed and in truth. And hereby we know that we are of the truth, and shall assure our hearts before Him."

Believers should help believers, should share with believers. We should bear one another's burdens. We should help each other financially when we see a brother in need. We should help each other in any way we can help our fellowman. This old world needs a baptism of real Christian love. Most Christians are entirely too selfish, too self-centered——and most of the time they think only of themselves.

The person who gives his money, his time, his energy in the things of the world and in fleshly interests is sure to reap corruption. But the person who invests time, money and energy in cultivating spiritual and heavenly things is sure to reap a heavenly harvest in life more abundant. In John 10:10 Jesus said, "I am come that they might have life, and that they might have it more abundantly."

These words should be pointed out here: "But this I say, He which soweth sparingly shall reap also sparingly; and he which soweth bountifully shall reap also bountifully. Every man according as he purposeth in his heart, so let him give; not grudgingly, or of necessity: for God loveth a cheerful giver. And God is able to make all grace abound toward you; that ye always having all sufficiency in all things, may abound to every good work: (As it is written, He hath dispersed abroad; he hath given to the poor: His righteousness remaineth for ever. Now he that ministereth seed to the sower both minister bread for your food, and multiply your seed sown, and increase the fruits of your righteousness;) Being enriched in every thing to all bountifulness, which causeth through us thanksgiving to God" (II Cor. 9:6—11).

The final reaping——the final harvest——will be when the Lord returns: "Be patient therefore, brethren, unto the coming of the Lord. Behold, the husbandman waiteth for the precious fruit of the earth, and hath long patience for it, until he receive the early and latter rain. Be ye also patient; stablish your hearts: for the coming of the Lord draweth nigh" (James 5:7—8). Also read Mark 4: 26—29.

In verse 10 of our chapter in Galatians, Paul is summing up the Law of Christ concerning *giving* and *doing* ––first and foremost to the Lord, and then to the brethren as they have need. When we walk in the Spirit, the Spirit will produce the fruit mentioned in Galatians 5: 22—23. When we love our fellowman as we should, we will not see him suffer if we are able to help him concerning the material things that have to do with the body. Christianity can be summed up in one short word: LOVE. God is love. We love Him because He first loved us. All the Law and the prophets hang on two commandments: (1) Love God with all your heart, mind, soul, strength; (2) Love your neighbor as yourself.

Verse 11: "Ye see how large a letter I have written unto you with mine own hand." The literal Greek reads, "Ye see with how large letters I have written unto you with mine own hand." Bible scholars believe the Apostle Paul was almost blind when he wrote the Galatian epistle. He was afflicted, and it is thought he had a disease of the eyes known as "ophthalmia," a disease quite prominent in the east at that time. Ordinarily, Paul dictated his letters, but the Galatian letter was written with his own hand. This is one of the most ––if not THE most important of the epistles the Holy Ghost dictated to Paul. He wrote with large letters–– big letters––because of his very poor eyesight.

Verse 12: "As many as desire to make a fair shew in the flesh, they constrain you to be circumcised; only lest they should suffer persecution for the cross of Christ." It seems the Galatians to whom Paul had preached the marvelous Grace of God——salvation by Grace through faith plus nothing——were like the Pharisees, the Scribes and the hypocrites in the days of Jesus. They wanted to make a fair show. "For ye are like unto whited sepulchres, which indeed appear beautiful outward, but are within full of dead men's bones, and of all uncleanness. Even so ye also outwardly appear righteous unto men, but within ye are full of hypocrisy and iniquity" (Matt. 23:27—28).

These scorching words were spoken by the Son of God, of whom the liberals like to preach as being a great God of love who would not permit anyone to be damned or to suffer! Paul rebukes the Galatians for desiring to make a fair show in the flesh. Man looks on the outward appearance, but God looks on the heart.

Verse 13: "For neither they themselves who are circumcised keep the Law; but desire to have you circumcised, that they may glory in your flesh."

Those who had disturbed the Galatian believers were seeking a great number of followers in order that they might be recognized as great leaders, great religionists. The same is true today. It is a common sin among religionists——and sad to say, also among some true believers——that they desire to build a reputation as great leaders, great ministers. Paul tells the Galatians the only reason the legalizers want them to be circumcised and practice the Law of Moses is simply that they "may glory in your flesh."

Verses 14 and 15: "But God forbid that I should glory, save in the cross of our Lord Jesus Christ, by whom the world is crucified unto me, and I unto the world. For in Christ Jesus neither circumcision availeth any thing, nor uncircumcision, but a new creature."

Paul had a singular subject. Regardless of where he preached, or to whom he preached, *he preached the message of the cross.* To the Corinthians he said, "I am determined not to know anything among you save Jesus Christ and Him crucified." To the Galatians he said, "God forbid that I should glory save in the cross of our Lord Jesus Christ, by whom the world is crucified unto me and I unto the world." To the Corinthians he said, "I preached unto you the Gospel, how that Christ died for our sins according to the Scriptures, was buried and rose again the third day *according to the Scriptures.*" Paul's message was a bloody message——the message of the cross, the message religionists today call "a butcherhouse message." I remind you that "without the shedding of blood there is no remission . . . ." "The blood of Jesus Christ, God's Son, cleanseth us from all sin . . . When I see the blood, I will pass over you!" So——it is blood, or hell. If you are not under the blood you stand spiritually naked, disgraced, and condemned before God; but if you are covered by the blood, you are just as just as Jesus is just in the sight of a Holy God. When God looks at you He sees the blood——and He honors the blood of His only begotten Son.

Paul summed up his testimony in Galatians 2:20: "I am crucified with Christ: nevertheless I live; yet not I, but Christ liveth in me: and the life which I now live in the flesh I live by the faith of the Son of God, who loved me, and gave Himself for me."

Verse 15 tells us, in literal language, "For neither is circumcision anything, nor uncircumcision anything, but a new creation." That is——except a man be born from above he cannot enter the kingdom of God. "Therefore if any man be in Christ, he is a new creature: old things are passed away; behold, all things are become new" (II Cor. 5:17).

Circumcision here represents formalism, legality, external religion having a form of godliness but denying the power thereof. There are many such people today. Read carefully II Timothy 3:5. Not only does such religion avail nothing, but such religion IS nothing. I pointed out earlier in this study that all we do, all we give, regardless of how great it may be, adds up to one big zero unless the love of God (Jesus Christ) abides in our bosom. The new creation through the miracle of the new birth is the only thing God honors. "We are His workmanship, created in Christ Jesus . . ." (Eph. 2:10a).

Verse 16: "And as many as walk according to this rule, peace be on them, and mercy, and upon the Israel of God." The rule to which Paul refers here was stated in verse 15 . . . the believer's perfect rule of life, a new creation in Christ Jesus, a new creature born from above, transformed by the power of God. Not circumcision--nor the lack of it. Not Law-keeping, not works, not religious formality--but a new creation in Christ Jesus. The believer has been made new from above, created anew in Christ. The true believer worships God in spirit and in truth, rejoicing in the Christ and not in the flesh. We are commanded to put no confidence in the flesh.

Does this mean that Christians should not do good works? God forbid! Indeed it does not. Faith that saves is *living* faith, and "faith without works is dead" (James 2:20). "Faith which worketh by love" (Gal. 5:6) is the faith that saves us. We have been created in Christ Jesus *unto* good works (Eph. 2:10), but good works referred to here are not Law-works, but sacrificial service to the Lord Jesus and to fellow believers. These works are not worked that we might be saved, but because we are already saved. We do not perform good works to keep saved, but we work good works because we are bone of His bone and flesh of His flesh (Eph. 5:30).

In our present verse, Paul refers to the Israel of God, which consists of the natural seed of Father Abraham, who of course are also spiritual: "For they are not all Israel, which are of Israel" (Rom. 9:6). Again, "He is not a Jew, which is one outwardly; neither is that circumcision, which is outward in the flesh: But he is a Jew, which is one inwardly; and circumcision is that of the heart, in the spirit, and not in the letter; whose praise is not of men, but of God" (Rom. 2:28—29). Also read and carefully study John 8:37—44.

Verse 17: "From henceforth let no man trouble me: for I bear in my body the marks of the Lord Jesus."

Paul had already defended his right to speak as an apostle. He clearly announced that God called him, ordained him, and sent him . . . and that God revealed the message he was to preach. And now he has ample proof that he told the truth when he announced his heavenly ordination. What is the proof? "FOR I BEAR IN MY BODY THE MARKS OF THE LORD JESUS!"

The Greek word for "marks" is a word that refers to the marks branded on slaves to indicate their owners. It was very common in the days of Paul. Paul's body bore the mark of circumcision——but this mark he declared was of no value. He then pointed to scars he had received in the fight of faith. He was proud of those scars, and he had a spiritual right to be proud of the scars he had received for the Gospel's sake. In his last moments on earth he testified, "For I am now ready to be offered, and the time of my departure is at hand. I have fought a good fight, I have finished my course, I have kept the faith: Henceforth there is laid up for me a crown of righteousness, which the Lord, the righteous judge, shall give me at that day: and not to me only, but unto all them also that love His appearing" (II Tim. 4:6—8).

Paul was a good soldier. He kept his guns loaded at all times. He received many battle-scars——but he came out victorious: *He received a crown!*

Verse 18: "Brethren, the grace of our Lord Jesus Christ be with your spirit. Amen."

The word "brethren" refers only to the true born again believers. All born again believers are brethren. All church members are not brethren, all men are not brothers in the spiritual sense . . . only the born again are "brethren."

In the II Corinthian epistle Paul closes by saying, "The grace of the Lord Jesus Christ, and the love of God, and the communion of the Holy Ghost, be with you all. Amen" (II Cor. 13:14). The "you all" in this verse applies only to the church, the born again. The Word of God does not make known any blessing whatsoever for those who reject the pure Gospel of God's grace. They tread the Son of God under their feet, they make the blood of the covenant an unholy thing, they do despite unto the Spirit of God's marvelous grace (Heb. 10:28—31). God pity them when they fall into the hands of the living God!

The marvelous Grace of God is for "ALL THEM THAT LOVE OUR LORD JESUS CHRIST IN SINCERITY" (Eph. 6:24).

To the enemies of the cross, enemies of the blood and the virgin-born, crucified, risen Christ, the Scriptures announce: "IF ANY MAN LOVE NOT OUR LORD JESUS CHRIST LET HIM BE ACCURSED. OUR LORD COMETH" (I Cor. 16:22).

"The wages of sin is death . . . when sin is finished

it bringeth forth death . . . God is angry with the wicked every day . . . the wicked shall be turned into hell, and all nations that forget God . . . But God commendeth His love toward us in that while we were yet sinners, Christ died for the ungodly."

It is not God's will that any perish, but that all come to repentance. Dear friend, if you are not born again, if you do not know the Grace of God, why not bow your head, confess your lost condition, invite Jesus to come into your heart. He will--and you will know it!

Paul closes: "THE GRACE OF THE LORD JESUS CHRIST BE WITH YOUR SPIRIT. AMEN." Grace is the KEY WORD of the Epistle to the Galatians. Paul declares plainly and without apology, salvation is by Grace, through faith, plus nothing! Not one thing can be given or wrought to save or to help save. Saved by Grace, kept by Grace, and God's marvelous Grace is multiplied to the recipients of Grace in the measure in which they believe the Word and walk IN the Word. We are born into the family of God instantaneously. We are commanded to grow in Grace and in the knowledge of our Lord and Saviour, Jesus Christ. We do not grow *into* Grace--we are *born* into Grace; but we grow in Grace AFTER Grace comes into our heart. Certainly the key word in the Epistle to the Galatians is "GRACE!" Paul, inspired of the Holy Ghost, wrote the Epistle to the Galatians and to all believers, in defense of salvation by Grace, through Faith, plus nothing. Thank God for Galatians!